Paul Johnson

"Get Writing!"

Creative book-making projects for children

Pembroke Publishers Limited

Pembroke Publishers
538 Hood Road
Markham, Ontario, Canada L3R 3K9
www.pembrokepublishers.com

Distributed in the U.S. by Stenhouse Publishers
480 Congress Street
Portland, ME 04101-3400
www.stenhouse.com

First published in 2005 by A & C Black Publishers Ltd
38 Soho Square, London W1D 3HB www.acblack.com

Library and Archives Canada Cataloguing in Publication

Johnson, Paul, 1943-
    Get writing! : creative book-making projects for children / Paul Johnson.

Includes index.
ISBN 1-55138-201-6

    1. Creative writing (Primary education) 2. Book design—Study and teaching (Primary) 3. Storytelling ability in children. I. Title.

LB1528.J64 2006   372.62'3   C2005-907190-7

The author and publisher would like to thank the staff and pupils of the following schools for their help with this project.
Birchfields Primary School, Manchester
St Augustine's Primary School, Manchester
Hursthead Infant School, Stockport
Offerton Hall Primary School, Stockport
North Baddesley Infant School, Southampton
Thorn Grove Primary School, Stockport
Castleview Primary School, Slough
North Baddesley Infant School, Southampton

For information on Paul Johnson's The Book Art Project visit www.bookart.co.uk

Literacy Consultant: Christine Moorcroft
Editor: Beck Ward-Murphy, Kate Revington
Design: HL Studios, JayTee Graphics

Printed and bound in Canada
9 8 7 6 5 4 3 2 1

Contents

THE PROJECTS

THE TEMPLATES

Introduction

Writing and drawing in a book that you have made yourself is magical. Writing can be a drag for some children, but practising it in their own book — especially one with pop-ups or lift-up flaps inside — takes the sting out of writing. Moreover, a book form provides a concrete base for organizing topics, putting things into categories, processing information and integrating text with illustration.

Children take pride in their school-made books and are eager to take them home and share them with their family and friends. One thing lost from primary education in recent times is this personal and social aspect of the learning process — the divorcing of skill acquisition from creative involvement. The projects in this book will engage children and give them the desire to write.

The projects

This book is organized into different projects. Each project starts with the basic book-making structure and then offers some variations. Each book form is not necessarily harder to make than its predecessor, so any of the book forms are appropriate at any stage of development. Likewise, the projects are not chronological in terms of writing difficulty, so determine which book ideas suit the themes of your current short- or medium-term planning and work from there.

Showing children how to fold

Go through the folding process slowly, repeating what to do at each stage. First, demonstrate folding with the class watching, and then again with the students copying you. Some students will understand quickly and others will take more time. Suggest that the students do the folding in pairs so they can help each other with any tricky bits. Always have spare paper at the ready for disasters and don't forget to reverse the instructions as necessary for left-handed children.

Making the books – who does what?

Some five-year-olds demonstrate better creative skills than children twice their age. They may pick up folding skills quickly and, in a relatively short time, fold with accuracy. The basic zigzag book and scissor-cutting skills are within the grasp of most young children, providing that simple step-by-step instructions are given. Repetition is essential to grasp these skills and develop further.

There are situations, however, when the time invested in book making will seem excessive and teacher/teacher assistant production becomes necessary. Where possible, timesaving folding and cutting methods are given under the heading "CUTTING MULTIPLES." This will allow you to make a book quickly, saving you time when preparing for the lesson. **Please note that these techniques are for you, not the children**. A compromise solution would be for you to do the initial folding, but for students to complete any folding and cutting.

Rough and finished models

Students can make a rough model of their book or pop-up on plain letter size paper before embarking on the finished piece. Use the practice piece for preparatory work or let students take it home to share with their family and friends.

Materials and equipment

PAPER

Photocopier paper is suitable for drafting, but I recommend that you use sturdier paper for finished work.

It's difficult to be prescriptive about paper size. With very young children, books from letter size paper can be too small — chunky crayons and broad strokes demand a larger format. Some six-year-olds, though, love working in tiny formats and large pages can sometimes daunt students. This book refers to these sizes:

- letter size – 21 cm × 28 cm (8 ½ in. × 11 in.)
- ledger size – 28 cm × 43 cm (11 in. × 17 in.)
- large size – 42 cm × 54 cm (18 in. × 24 in.)
- poster size – 60 cm × 84 cm (22 in. × 34 in.)

In some cases, the nature of the project itself will suggest the size of paper to use. Sizes are approximate.

TOOLS

For most of the projects, all you need is scissors and, occasionally, rulers and glue. Glue sticks are suitable for rough models on thin paper, but white glue is best for thicker paper and pop-ups. Project 18 will need a long-arm stapler, and projects 20 and 21 ideally use a bookbinder's awl.

When you are making books for children, a craft knife cutting along a steel ruler will produce better results than using scissors. You can also cut multiples more quickly.

Be sure to advise the class about using scissors safely:

- Keep the scissors shut when not in use.
- Hold the paper you are cutting below the scissor-cutting direction.
- Make sure that the scissors are not hidden under any pieces of paper while working.

ART MATERIALS

For the youngest children, provide pencils and a range of crayons, progressing to colored pens and pencils for drawing. Photographs, collage and computer-generated material can be used as alternatives to original artwork.

Writing

I have suggested shared writing and writing frame techniques where appropriate. In general, tasks need to build on one another. In the first project, for example, younger students make marks representing doors and windows and progress to labelling: "door," "window," etc. Then simple captions emerge. "My house" becoming "This is my house," and then more complex sentences, such as "In my kitchen you will find an oven and a fridge." One unique feature of the basic zigzag book is that it can be folded so that only one page is visible. Sequencing, then, is controlled so that students work within a specific area, one page at a time.

Drafting and writing preparations are relevant surprisingly early on. While immediacy is essential at early stages of writing, by six years of age children should do some form of drafting. The drafting method described below is unique to the book-making approach for teaching writing.

HIDDEN DRAFTING BOOKS

1. Make the basic zigzag book and number the pages 1–4.

2. Open the back of the book upwards. Then fold the top edge of the paper forwards to the halfway crease.

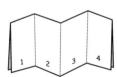

3. Fold the top edge forward again and number the pages 1–4. Students can use these pages for draft work and present their finished work on the bottom panels.

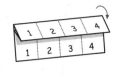

4. When finished, open out the paper and make the basic book again. Students can use the top part of the page for illustrations.

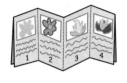

The advantages of this drafting technique are that the draft cannot be lost, it is immediately adjacent to the presented work, it's hidden from view and it can be instantly accessed for assessment purposes by both you and the student.

Use writing frames where necessary by adding a frame on each of the drafting pages (e.g., "This is my . . ."). Open the sheet and photocopy the writing-frame side for each student. Fold each copy up to make a hidden drafting book. Students can complete the writing frame prefix and copy the sentence onto the page below it. After refolding the book, they draw pictures in the top half of each page to complete the task.

Style

Writing, pictures and diagrams look so much better if contained within borders. Make card templates 2 cm (³/₄ in.) smaller than the dimensions of the page from discarded boxes, such as cornflake packets. Students can put these in the middle of the page and draw around them to create borders.

Making your own instruction book

Using any of the book forms on pages 6–7, design your own writing frames, headings and captions for class projects. Don't forget that the top panels must be prepared upside down to the bottom panels. Remember to leave generous margins, especially to the outer edges.

Displaying work

Books are for looking at and for reading. Some of the projects in this book have work solely on the front four pages so that the whole is visible when attached to a display surface. Experiment with different vertical, horizontal and diagonal patterns of arranging the books children make. Where possible, integrate published books into the display so that children can see themselves as part of a tradition and a culture that goes back hundreds, even thousands of years.

Making the basic books

The zigzag book

The eight-page zigzag book — the easiest of all books to make, for it requires nothing other than one sheet of paper — is the basis for many of the projects in this book. In its simplest four-page form, it can be used in an infinite number of ways: portraying four family members, retelling a traditional story in four episodes, presenting reflective poems on the four seasons, describing four favorite toys or recounting four highlights of a visit to a farm. Of course, the book can be used on its reverse side also, but remember to reserve pages for the cover. Furthermore, doors and flaps that open on the page can provide more areas for captioned diagrams or text — only a pair of scissors is required.

1. Fold a sheet of letter size paper in half widthways, from right to left (or the other way if left handed).

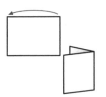

2. Turn the sheet to the landscape position and then fold in half widthways again, from right to left (or the other way if left handed). Unfold once.

3. Keeping the paper landscape, fold the top edge to the bottom edge and then unfold the whole sheet fully.

4. Fold the sheet lengthways in half and zigzag the pages into a book.

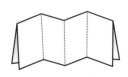

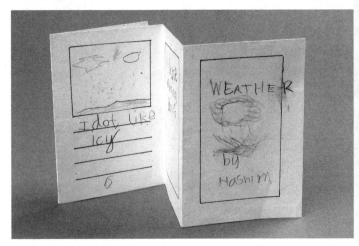

"Weather" by Hashim (aged 5). Hashim describes a different type of weather on each of the four front panels of this zigzag book: cloudy, sunny, etc. The first panel on the back is for weather he likes and the second one for weather he doesn't like. The final two panels are the front and back cover.

The origami book

An offshoot from a simple zigzag book is what is commonly known as an origami book. By making a single cut to the basic zigzag book, and by using a different folding pattern, a fantastic three-spread book is created.

1. Open the zigzag book and fold it widthways in half. On the folded edge, make a cut on the horizontal crease.

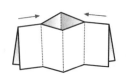

2. Open out the whole sheet and fold it lengthways in half. Push the left and right edges all the way into the centre to make a cross.

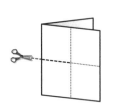

3. Fold up the pages, as shown, to make the book.

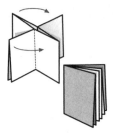

The four-page book

As an alternative to the eight-page zigzag or origami book, you can make a book with fewer pages but with larger page dimensions. It is a matter of choosing which of these two basic book forms best suits the project to go inside it.

1. Using a sheet of paper in portrait position, fold the top edge down to the bottom edge. Unfold.

2. Fold the right edge to the left edge (fold the other way if left handed). Unfold.

3. Make a cut on the left edge along the horizontal crease.

4. Fold the paper horizontally in half. Then fold the front left-hand panel forwards and the back left-hand panel backwards, to make the book.

"Our Playground" by Adam (aged 6). The students were engaged in redesigning their playground. The left pages of this four-page book illustrate and describe what games and activities are already available there. Each right page is a projection: "What I would like to be able to play."

Making a basic book template

Prepare lines for writing and boxes for pictures or diagrams in advance. Templates for the eight-page zigzag book and the origami book are on pages 60 and 61; the four-page book is on page 62. Photocopy the templates onto letter size paper or enlarge them if you prefer. As students develop their writing skills, use one book as a draft (with picture areas left blank for your comments and the student's editing) and the other for the presented work.

A teacher-designed number book: A teacher has made her own small-scale origami instruction book and photocopied it for the whole class. Students trace over the words and color in the illustrations.

Book covers

Try the following centring technique (also a good math game) to help children space the lettering on their book covers: (1) Draw a line down the centre of the book's cover; (2) write the middle letter, or imagine the space between the middle letters, of the title and the author's name on the middle line; (3) write forwards to finish the word and backwards to the beginning of the word.

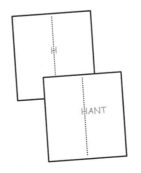
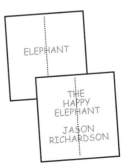

Making books and literacy

Get Writing! promotes the development of important writing and numeracy skills.

First of all, the book-making projects featured in this book develop the numeracy skills of measuring and of solving problems. They also develop the children's awareness of the characteristics of planes and solid shapes and of patterns and spaces. Many of them require children to count; their attention could be drawn to the number of squares or oblongs in the net for a book, or the number of rows and how many are in each row. You will also find opportunities for focusing on fractions: for example, directions might call for paper to be folded in half or in quarters.

This teaching resource encourages children to write for pleasure and to develop essential and varied writing skills.

You will find opportunities for making books related to the study of English, mathematics, science, history, geography, art & design, citizenship, religious education, and design & technology. The projects can be easily adapted to apply to many themes and subjects.

The books the children create call for different kinds of writing, both fiction and non-fiction. In general, children gain practice in writing captions and labels, short reports, recounts, retellings, rhymes, character studies, and more.

The table below outlines in specific detail the types of writing and themes that each chapter suggests in its USE IT! activities.

Book	Types of writing	Notes on themes
1 – Shape books: Buildings	Captions, labels, lists, story retellings, non-fiction texts, recounts, non-chronological reports, descriptions of setting, alternative endings, sequels for known stories	Children can explore animal habitats, different buildings in the neighborhood, the role of houses in familiar stories, the nature of homes now and long ago, and more exotic settings.
2 – Shape books: People	Captions, simple non-fiction books, reports, character profiles and sketches	Children write about family members, people who help them in their communities, the work that someone in a particular role does, characters from myth, history, personal life, and story, as well as about the food that people eat.
3 – Topsy-turvy books	Simple picture storybooks, extended captions, questions, information, descriptions of story settings, non-fiction, non-chronological reports	These shape books lend themselves to stories about car trips, magical and normal; factual information about creatures, such as frogs; back-and-forth letter writing between characters, such as Goldilocks and Baby Bear; and question and answer exchanges.
4 – Palaces, pyramids and more!	Captions, labels, character sketches and profiles, non-chronological reports, descriptions, evaluations, lists	These projects prompt children to explore palaces as they figure in fairy tales and in history, as well as pyramids and their contents. Children can even develop the books into festive cards for celebrations, such as Christmas, and fancy party planners.
5 – Castle books	Captions; labels; lists; story retellings; descriptions, including of settings; non-chronological reports	Can buildings speak? Like palace books, castle books let students work with traditional stories set in castles. Children can also learn more about castle life in the Middle Ages, or make a mosque to focus on a religious festival.
6 – Contour books	Captions, labels, character sketches and profiles, non-fiction, questions	These books let students explore choices and alternatives, such as those related to citizenship and science concepts such as light and dark.
7 – Fold-away books	Postcards/letters, fantasy, simple picture storybooks, lists, labels, notes, story retellings, rhymes as models for writing, descriptions of setting, information, as for a menu	These vertical zigzag books permit writing related to different kinds of houses and stores, ranging from a witch's candy house to a grandfather clock to a four-level home.
8 – Animal books 1	Simple picture storybooks, using known stories as models; questions; recounts; non-fiction; non-chronological reports	Children can write about animals in terms of dairy products, protection of endangered species, and Santa Claus's reindeer. Both science and citizenship themes can be developed with these animal books.

9 – Animal books 2	Labels, captions, non-fiction, non-chronological reports, simple picture storybooks, collation of information	Different-shaped animals, such as dinosaurs and elephants, can become the focus for studies about variation, specific creatures, and our relationships with animals.
10 – Pocket folders	Labels, captions, notes, letters, messages, lists	This project integrates a range of writing genres presented as removable objects in a pocket folder or an origami wallet: these might range from birthday cards to to-do lists.
11 – Folded cards	Character sketches and profiles, simple stories in familiar settings, questions and captions, descriptions of setting	Children can create the exteriors and interiors of places, such as what's behind a door, places of worship, a rainforest and the animals within it.
12 – Surprise cards	Notes, letters, messages, character sketches, promotional writing, collaborative writing	Pop-up "theatre" cards are ideal for developing a focus on family celebrations and religious festivals.
13 – Theatre books	Simple picture storybooks, character studies, retellings of story incidents, recounts, non-chronological reports, descriptions of settings, explorations of main issues of stories, alternative endings for known stories	Toy theatre books allow children to create 3D dramatic scenes, write about stories or myths on the panels, and experiment with the potential of different panel styles. They adapt well for writing about special celebrations.
14 – Pop-up theatres	Labels, signs, simple picture storybooks, retellings of known stories, play scripts, dialogues, conversations, alternative endings for known stories	Like the other theatres, these pop-ups provide great stimuli for writing. They can also be developed into theatre books that retell familiar stories. Children could also focus on historical individuals and special faith days.
15 – Backdrop pop-ups	Writing about settings, play scripts, lists, messages, promotional writing, first-person writing, labels, captions, instructions	Backdrop pop-ups leave much room for writing. Children could explore geographical themes, such as aspects of the local neighborhood or the tropics, or citizenship issues, such as living in a diverse world.
16 – Tower pop-ups	Labels, captions, messages, notes, lists, letters, retellings of stories, collaborative stories, descriptions of settings, myths, legends	Tower pop-ups work well for exploring themes of health and growth. They also provide opportunities for students to make and list choices, such as healthy and unhealthy foods.
17 – Puzzle books	Character sketches, captions, questions, lists, descriptions of scenes, use of writing frames	A variety of puzzle books provide students with options for making pictures, captions and labels about buildings, plants and animals, and local and faraway geographical settings.
18 – Invisible-join books	Alphabetical lists, labels, captions, instructions, rules, poetry using simple structures, new or extended verses for known poems, riddles, rhymes	Activities promote making choices. For example, students write about what would make their school a happy place.
19 – Books with covers	Labels, captions, non-fiction, instructions, questions and answers	Students can write about plants, animals, the seasons, and their communities.
20 – Sewn books	Simple non-fiction, non-chronological reports, recounts, retellings of stories	Bound books enable the class to preserve work that they produce collaboratively; they are suitable for non-fiction report writing and recounts.
21 – Side-bound books	Extended stories, glossaries, dictionaries, alphabetical directories; also, collaborative writing (fiction and non-fiction)	These sewn books work well for large-scale sheets of children's artwork or compilations of work on a given theme.
22 – Accordion books	Extended stories, non-fiction, writing sequences, collaborative writing	Flexible accordion books are useful for presenting whole-class or group work.
23 – Stories in boxes	Retellings of known stories, simple stories	Story boxes encourage all kinds of fiction writing.
24 – Lotus books	Labels, captions, messages, notes, character portraits, lists	Decorative and versatile, lotus books are a great impetus for the study of celebrations such as Chinese New Year.
25 – Firework books	Labels, simple poetry structures, new or extended verses for known poems, descriptions, riddles, alphabets	Children can explore shapes and patterns.

1 – Shape books: Buildings

Children associate strongly with buildings. After all, their home, their friends' homes and their school are probably all buildings. In these shape books, each page can represent a different building or part of a building, e.g., a row of shops or the rooms in a house.

Make the basic buildings book

1. Fold a ledger sheet of paper in half lengthways. Then fold it up into a zigzag book.

2. Cut off the top corners of each page.

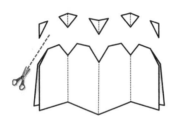

CUTTING MULTIPLES
Fold the book into a zigzag. Cut off all the left corners simultaneously and then all the right corners.

USE IT!

- On the first page, draw a building and write a caption, e.g., "This is my house." Continue with different buildings and captions on the remaining pages. Write a title for the book on the front cover.

Buildings with doors

1. Make the basic buildings book, then open the sheet and cut out some doors. Cut only two sides for each door — don't cut them out completely.

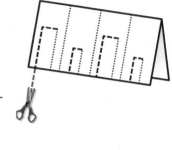

2. Fold the sheet back up and open the doors.

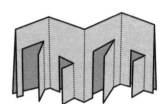

★ Helpful hint: If you're unsure, try it on a piece of scrap paper first.

USE IT!

- Use the panels to show different animal habitats, e.g., a mouse in a hole, a dog in a kennel. Vary the sizes of the doors.

- "Who's behind the door?" Can you guess? Open the door to reveal the name of a person or an animal written on the inside of the flap and a drawing of the subject through the door.

- Label the panels as different stores, for instance, a sweet shop, a toy store, or a post office. Open the door and write a list of what each store offers.

Buildings with regularly shaped doors

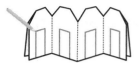

1. Make the basic buildings book. Draw a door in the centre of each panel.

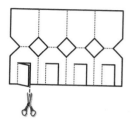

2. Open the sheet and cut out the doors.

3. Fold the sheet back up to make the finished book.

CUTTING MULTIPLES

1. After cutting off the corners, open the sheet and fold it in half widthways.

2. Fold the edges back to the vertical crease. Cut all the doors simultaneously through the bottom panels. Fold them forward and backward.

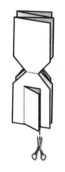

3. Open the whole sheet and then fold it back up to make the book.

"The Three Little Pigs" by Sam (aged 7). For this project, the teacher gave the beginning of the first sentence to be completed by the students – "Mother Pig said to her three children…."After the drafting stage, it was written inside the first door. The story unfolds on the remaining pages in a similar fashion.

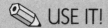 USE IT!

- Retell the story of "The Three Little Pigs" in four parts: mother pig's house, the straw house, the wooden house and the brick house. The children draw a house on the outside and write the episodes on the inside.

- Make a house book. The children draw a room through each open door, for example, a kitchen, and list the contents of the room on the back of the door.

- Adopt a writing frame: "I would like to be …" Write a sentence on each door and draw a self-portrait in the appropriate setting inside, for example, an astronaut in a rocket, a nurse in a hospital.

Buildings and objects

Starting with the basic buildings book, cut an outline as shown. Remember to leave a part of the top of each page uncut. Then decide where to cut the doors.

USE IT!

- For a space adventure, draw a house on the first page, a rocket on the second, a space station on the third and a house on the fourth. Write a space adventure story inside the doors.

For example:

1. This is Martha …
2. Martha took off in her …
3. She went to a party on the moon and …
4. When she came home she …

2 – Shape books: People

Creating people-shaped books makes projects about people you admire or food you eat more interesting. Adding flaps gives extra pages for more text or for drawing diagrams.

Make the basic people book

1. Make the basic buildings book (see page 10).

2. Cut out a head and shoulders shape on each of the panels.

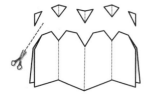

IMPORTANT: Do not cut out the top part of the head or your book will fall apart!

CUTTING MULTIPLES

Make the basic book. Keeping it closed, cut one head and shoulders shape, going through all the panels at the same time.

What people do

1. Make the basic buildings book. Cut the corners off the first panel and a head and shoulders shape from the second panel.

2. Repeat steps 1 and 2 for panels three and four.

✏️ USE IT!

- The children draw a member of their family on the first panel of the book. Beneath the picture, ask them to write something about the person such as, "This is my mom. She likes going for walks and drinking bottled water." These family portraits can be continued up to page four and onto the other side of the book if desired.

✏️ USE IT!

- Discuss people who do jobs that help us in our daily lives, such as a firefighter. The children can draw and caption a fire station on the first panel of their book and the firefighter on the second panel. Ask them to select another job and another place of work for the remaining panels.

- Talk about the different tasks a person does from day to day. Make a people book with head and shoulder shapes cut out on panel 1 and the corners cut off the remaining panels. The children could then plan out their book as follows: a gardener on panel 1, a garden on panel 2, a garden shed on panel 3 and a greenhouse on panel 4.

- Using the basic people book, you might draw biblical characters Mary, Joseph and Jesus on one side of the book. Use two other basic people books to show the shepherds and the wise ones. After drawing pictures and writing captions on each panel, the children can separate the panels by cutting and arrange them into a nativity scene.

Note: If making the nativity book, cut a head and shoulders on all of the panels.

Lift-the-flap people!

Make the basic people book. Open out the book fully and cut four flaps. Then fold the sheet back into the book again, ready for use.

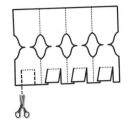

CUTTING MULTIPLES

1. Make the basic people book using the cutting multiples method. Open up the book and fold in half widthways.

2. Fold the edges to the vertical crease. Make two parallel cuts, as shown.

3. Fold the panels forward and back. Unfold.

4. Open the whole sheet. Finally, fold it back to make a zigzag book.

✎ USE IT!

- Get the class thinking about food: food they like, food they don't like and food that they think is good for them. On page 1 of their book, ask them to draw a head and then, under the flap, one of their favorite foods. They can add a caption to the outside of the flap, such as "I like ..." and complete it on the inside of the flap. Repeat with other favorite foods on pages 2 to 4.

- Or, for variety, under the first two flaps draw and label healthy food – fruit, salad and vegetables. Use the last two flaps for junk food.

Arms and legs!

As this book involves a lot of cutting, I suggest that you make it for the children who then write in and illustrate.

1. Holding a sheet of paper in the landscape position, fold the top edge down to about 3 cm (1 ⅛ in.) from the bottom edge.

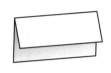

2. Fold the paper in half widthways, keeping the shorter section on the outside. Then fold the edges back to meet the vertical centre crease.

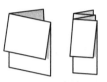

3. Cut out a simple figure. Take care not to cut across the top of the head, and ensure that the length of the legs is no more than about two fingers wide.

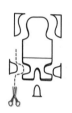

4. Next, open out the whole sheet. Fold it widthways in half once, and then in half again. Cut small flaps, as shown.

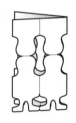

5. Open out the whole sheet again. Fold it along the horizontal crease and zigzag the pages back into the book form.

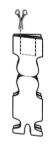

★ Helpful hint: Cut-out body accessories, like hats and scarves, can be added to the heads of the people using glue.

3 – Topsy-turvy books

The centre pages of this book contain artwork and the outer pages are used for writing. With these projects, you can focus on motivating possibly reluctant boy writers by using an exciting object, such as a car. Turned upside-down it becomes something else — an animal's head! — thus providing an interesting twist to the book and a new range of thematic possibilities.

Make the basic car book

Using the basic zigzag book, draw and cut out the outline of a car, as shown. Then fold the paper back into the book shape.

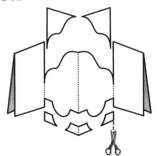

CUTTING MULTIPLES

Make the basic zigzag book and fold it widthways in half. Cut half a car shape on the folded edge. Unfold and then fold the paper back into the book shape.

★ Helpful hint: The wheels of the car should form part of the base of the book.

✎ USE IT!

- Draw the details of the car on both sides of the centre panels. Write a narrative on the side panels of both sides of the book. Example:

Panel 1: I am driving in my red car.

Panel 2: I am going to …

Panel 3: When I get there I will …

Panel 4: When I get home I will …

Give your car some scenery

1. Make the basic zigzag book using regular paper. Open out the whole sheet and fold it widthways in half. Cut half a car shape in the bottom centre panel.

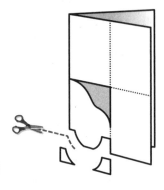

2. Open out the sheet again and fold it lengthways in half to make it into the book.

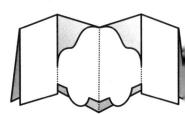

✎ USE IT!

- Draw the car and some people sitting inside it. Draw the scenery on the panels behind. Write a list of the car's passengers on the left panel, and then describe where they are going on the right panel.

- Give the class a project entitled "The Magic Car." Ask them to think about what makes their car magic and to list what magical things it can do on pages 1 and 4 of their book.

Goldilocks and Baby Bear

Make the basic car book, as before, but with the car shape upside down — we are going to turn the car into a bear!

CUTTING MULTIPLES

Make the basic car book using the cutting multiples method on page 14, but with the car shape upside down.

✏️ USE IT!

- Make sure that the children are familiar with the story of Goldilocks and the Three Bears. Ask them to draw a picture of Baby Bear on the two front centre panels. The writing project is as follows: Goldilocks writes to apologize for breaking Baby Bear's chair. The children should put this letter on the front left panel. Baby Bear replies on the front right panel. The correspondence can continue on the other side of the book.

- Ask the children to write a set of questions that they would like to ask Baby Bear on page 1. For example: What food does he like other than porridge? They put Baby Bear's replies on page 4. They can add pictures as they wish to match the text.

- The children list things that can be learned from the story of Goldilocks: Always lock your house; do not go into another person's house unless you are invited.

Correspondence between Goldilocks and Baby Bear by Frayah (aged 5). This letter-writing project exemplifies the first suggestion in USE IT! above. The writing frame was: Dear Baby Bear, I am sorry that I ... Yours sincerely, Goldilocks.

Frogs

Use this project for an introduction to frogs.

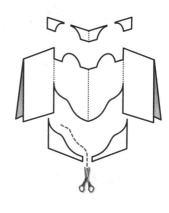

1. Make the basic car book again with the car shape upside down. This time, we're using the car shape to make a frog's head!

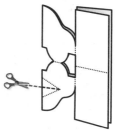

2. Open out the paper and fold it widthways in half. Make a horizontal cut on the bottom shaped panel.

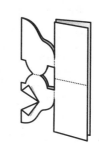

3. Crease angles forward and backward to make a mouth. Unfold.

4. Open the paper and fold it lengthways in half. Next, fold it into a zigzag and then raise the pop-up mouth, as shown.

CUTTING MULTIPLES

Make the basic zigzag book and fold it widthways in half. Cut out an upside-down car shape on the folded edge. Unfold and continue as from step 2 above.

✏️ USE IT!

- Ask the children to write about how frogs have sticky pads on their toes to help them climb. What else can they write about them?

- Children can draw a frog's face on pages 2 and 3 – the middle panels – to give their work an illustration.

4 – Palaces, pyramids and more!

These projects can be used as a focus for imaginary or historical buildings. They have triangular shapes as the cut-away design and the option of extra writing panels on each side.

Make the basic palace book

Make the basic zigzag book using ledger size paper. Cut away the triangles. Zigzag the pages back into the book, ready for use.

CUTTING MULTIPLES

Make the basic zigzag book as above and then fold it widthways in half. Cut out the triangles from the folded edge and then open the book ready for use.

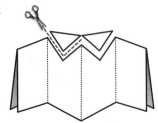

Party planner

1. Make the basic palace book, then open out the paper fully and cut side flaps.

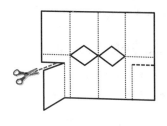

2. Fold the paper in half lengthways to complete the book.

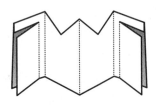

CUTTING MULTIPLES

Make the basic palace book using the cutting multiples technique. Open out the paper fully and then fold it in half widthways. Cut the side flaps. Unfold and then fold it lengthways to make the finished book.

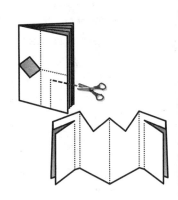

✏️ USE IT!

- Make sure that the class is familiar with the story of Cinderella. Ask them to draw Cinderella dressed in rags cleaning a house on the centre pages of one side. List her cleaning chores on the pages either side of the illustration.

- The children now turn their book over to the other side. Again, in the centre pages they draw Cinderella, this time dressed in party clothes at the palace ball. They could describe what she is wearing on the pages either side.

✏️ USE IT

- It's party time! Children can draw a paper-style party hat above a smiling face on pages 2 and 3 (the middle panels) of their books. On the side panels they could write a list of invited friends, games to play, a menu, a birthday cake recipe, or an invitation.

- Use the book as a holiday card. Draw a symbolic pattern in the centre, such as hearts or a wreath. On the inside flaps write an appropriate greeting or wish.

Camping

1. Make the palace book. Make the centre panels a pyramid shape. Open out fully and cut up the centre crease to create two tent flaps.

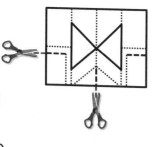

2. Fold the flaps outward, as shown. Cut two doors on the right and left panels.

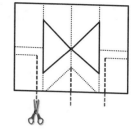

3. Fold the paper back in half lengthways and then zigzag the pages to make the finished book.

Cutting multiples

Use the same technique as for the party planner project, but make it a tent shape. Cut out the tent flaps as well as the side doors.

✎ USE IT!

- Draw a scene depicting "Me and My Best Friend" through the central flap of the tent. Open the left-hand door and write in a list of things you might take on holiday, such as your passport, a map, your swimsuit, a bat, a ball, your sandals. Under the right-hand door, children could add a smaller picture and label it, for example, a first-aid kit with content labels – bandages, sticky plasters, sunscreen, witch hazel.

★ Helpful hint: You don't need to keep to the designs suggested here. Invent your own shapes and combine any of the book forms!

Ancient Egypt

1. Make the basic pyramid book as for the Camping project but make the central flaps larger.

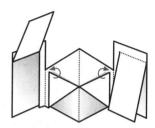

2. Cut the flaps on pages 1 and 4 so they lift upwards. Then fold the paper into the book, ready for use.

✎ USE IT!

- Use this project as a pyramid when learning about Egypt. The class draws an Egyptian mummy under the central flaps of their pyramid. Ask the children to think about items placed in pharaohs' tombs for the journey to the next life, such as pots of gold and statues. The tops of the flaps (pages 1 and 4) can be used for writing about these items.

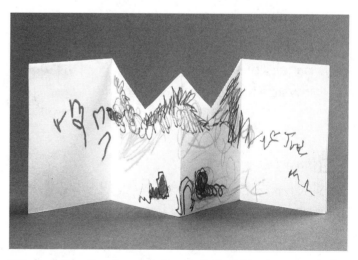

"Cinderella" by Zara (aged 4). Zara is distinguishing between which marks represent words (side panels) and which marks are pictorial (centre panels). In the foreground of the palace she has drawn the coach and horses.

5 – Castle books

Castles figure significantly in traditional stories and in Western history. By drawing both the inside and the outside, children learn about how castles were made and what it was like to live inside one.

Make the basic castle book

1. Make the basic zigzag book and open it out fully. Fold in half widthways and make a cut horizontally on the centre crease.

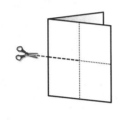

2. Open out the paper to the landscape position again and fold it lengthways in half. Cut rectangles from the top edges of the two centre panels, cutting through the double thickness of the paper.

3. Holding the left and right panels, push the paper inwards to make a tower.

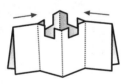

CUTTING MULTIPLES

Follow step 1, as above. Then, fold the paper in half from top to bottom and cut a rectangle out of the centre of the open top edge.

Unfold the paper fully and, in the landscape position, fold it lengthways in half. Then follow step 3, as above.

★ Helpful hint: Sharply re-crease the vertical folds of the castle so it stands upright more easily.

✏ USE IT!

- Tell the story of Jack and the Beanstalk. Each student draws a beanstalk growing around the castle walls and draws in a door with a giant in front of it. Write "This is the giant" on one of the side pages. The other panels can be used for recounting what happens after the giant wakes up.

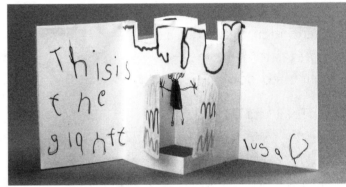

"Jack and the Beanstalk" by Lusa (aged 5). A teaching assistant cut out the shapes and did the main folding of the book for the whole class. Students did the final folding of the castle themselves and drew the giant through the open door.

Rapunzel

Follow steps 1–3 as for making the basic castle book. Hold the castle's middle front pages together and cut out a window.

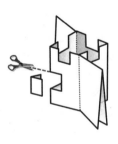

CUTTING MULTIPLES

Follow the instructions as for cutting multiple basic castle books, then unfold once and cut out the window.

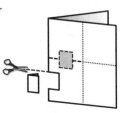

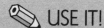

- On a spare piece of paper, the children can draw and cut out a picture of Rapunzel, glue on yellow wool for her long hair, and then glue her to the back of the window and let her hair fall down over the front of the castle. On the pages they can write the scene where Rapunzel is letting down her hair.

- Omit the rectangles from the top of the castle. The castle is now a tree trunk. Flatten the trunk and draw a tree-living animal, such as a bird or a squirrel, through the opening. Add writing frames on the left and right panels about the animals drawn.

Sleeping Beauty

1. Follow the steps for cutting multiple basic castle books. Hold the front centre panels of the castle together. Carefully cut the top and bottom of a door.

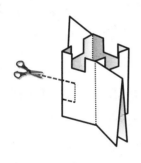

2. Cut the crease in the centre of the door, as shown, and fold back the flaps.

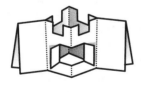

CUTTING MULTIPLES

Follow the steps for cutting multiple basic castle books. Lift up the front bottom panel and cut the top and bottom of the door. Unfold the paper and make the castle as above. Finally, cut the crease in the centre of the door and open it up.

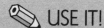

- Read the story of Sleeping Beauty to the class. Ask the children to flatten their castle books and draw Beauty through the open door, asleep on her bed. Draw the prince on the outside climbing up the wall. Use the side panels for retelling the scene.

- Omit the rectangles from the top of the castle to make a mosque. Through the door, draw a geometrical pattern and write a greeting on pages 1 and 4 of what can be an Eid card celebrating the end of the fast of Ramadan.

Castle banquet

Make the Sleeping Beauty castle book but cut a larger door in pages 2 and 3. Cut archway openings and battlements on pages 1 and 4.

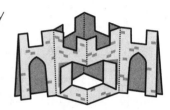

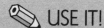

- Provide books with pictures showing what a medieval banquet looked like. Note the different things going on: food being brought to the tables, musicians strumming, the lord and lady of the castle eating, children playing. Ask the children to draw a large feasting table laid out with food and drink through the castle doors. In the left archway they can list some items from the feast with more pictures underneath, perhaps of someone eating the food. In the right archway they can list the games medieval children played and draw a picture of some children playing underneath.

★ Helpful hint: Experiment with ways of pinning pages 1 and 4 of the book to a display board so that the castle shape stays three-dimensional.

6 – Contour books

The format of these books allows you to present artwork as a panoramic view with a contoured edge at the top of the book. It is a novel visual feature designed to act as a stimulus for children's writing.

Make the basic contour book

1. Make the basic zigzag book and open it out fully. Fold the two short edges into the centre. Make two cuts on the folded edges, as shown.

2. Unfold the paper fully. Fold it lengthways in half and zigzag the pages, keeping the cut-out holes of the contours at the back of the book.

CUTTING MULTIPLES

Make the basic zigzag book and open it out fully. Fold the paper widthways and zigzag. Cut a slit on the side that has two folded edges.

✏️ USE IT!

- Children draw a wizard on the left-hand side of the book. On the right-hand side they write a spell, drawing and labelling the different ingredients needed.

- Clowns: Make a quarter-circle cut instead of a straight one. When folded this becomes the bowler hat of a clown on both sides. Students draw the hats and the clowns' heads – one happy and the other sad – and give them names. They could write a narrative explaining why one clown is sad and the other one happy.

★ Helpful hint: Use the wizard's hat idea on a large sheet of paper for a linked artwork lesson.

"The Witch" by Haris (aged 5). The class had been reading *Winnie in Winter* (Korky Paul & Valerie Thomas, OUP, 1996). They then made their own version of the book. The left side shows winter (falling snow) and the right side shows summer (bright sunshine).

Pop-up diamond

1. Make the basic zigzag book and open it out fully. Fold the right-hand shorter edge into the centre and make a cut.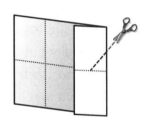

2. Fold the cut section of paper at an angle forwards and backwards. Unfold the paper fully.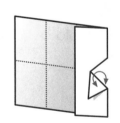

3. Fold the paper back into a zigzag book. The pop-up will fold in between pages 3 and 4 as you close the book, but pop up again as a diamond when you open it.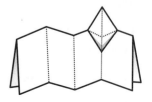

- Ask the children to think about what the diamond shape could be used for, such as a kite. They could write a story about the journey of a kite on the first two pages of the book and then draw the kite on the other two.

- Use the diamond as a star. The children can write a poem about what the star can see when it looks down to Earth: "I am a star. From the sky I can see …"

- Use the pop-up diamond as a flower head. The children draw petals, a stalk, leaves and roots and label them. On the left-hand spread they write a description of how plants or flowers start life as seeds.

Squares, triangles and circles

1. Follow step 1 for making the basic contour book, but cut the paper as shown on the right.

2. Open out the paper fully and fold it widthways in half. Make a cut as shown.

3. Open out the paper again. Fold it lengthways in half and zigzag the pages, keeping the cut-out holes of the contours at the back.

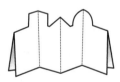

- Get the class thinking about shapes. Ask them to draw a square object in the first contour shape, such as a birthday present, and to list other square objects underneath. They then do the same with the other shapes.

- Discuss *habitats* with the children. They can draw a brick house in the first contour, a teepee in the second and an igloo in the third. Ask the children to write about who might live in these houses and also what materials they are made from.

Day and night

1. Follow step 1 for making the basic contour book, but cut two semi-circles as shown.

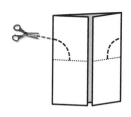

2. Open out the paper fully. Fold it lengthways in half and zigzag the book, keeping the cut-out holes of the contours at the back.

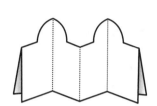

★ Helpful hint: To make accurate semi-circles, draw around a protractor or tin lid.

CUTTING MULTIPLES

1. Make the basic zigzag book. Open it out fully and fold it into a zigzag. Make a semi-circle cut on the edge with two folds.

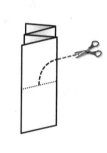

2. Open the sheet out fully, fold it lengthways in half and zigzag it to make up the book.

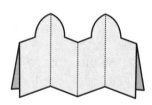

- In the four quarters of the first circle, the class draws objects associated with daytime: the sun, daytime birds, opened flowers, children playing outside. In the other circle, they should draw night-time objects: the moon, stars, an owl, children in bed. They can use the areas under the illustrations to write descriptions of what they've drawn.

7 – Fold-away books

These vertical zigzag books can be used in several contexts and, when displayed, are a pleasing alternative to more familiar horizontal books.

Make the basic fold-away book

1. Open out the basic zigzag book and cut it lengthways in half.

2. Hold one of the strips in the portrait position. Cut the corners from the top edge and fold the paper back up into the book, ready for use.

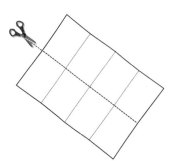

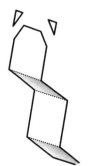

Holiday postcard wallet

1. Make the basic fold-away book. Next, make a cut on the third panel of the book, as shown. Open out the paper fully.

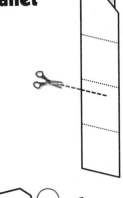

2. Fold the book into a wallet and "lock" page 1 into the slot on the back of page 3.

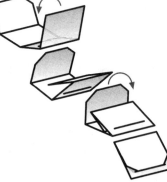

✏️ USE IT!

- Ask the class to imagine that they own a toy store and make a list of things to sell inside it. They should draw and caption different categories on the four levels of the store, such as indoor and outdoor toys or small and big toys.

- Tell the class that the book is a menu. Students draw a restaurant in the top panel, then list the starters, main courses and desserts in the remaining panels. What foods can they put in each of the three sections?

- The book is a house with a cellar, a ground floor, a first floor and an attic. Ask the class to draw and label the things they would find on each level of the house.

✏️ USE IT!

- Children can write four different holiday postcards to friends, e.g., "This morning I went ..." and "This afternoon I am going to ..."

- Ask the class to visualize the book as a grandfather clock. They can draw a clock face on the top panel and a mouse lower down. The narrative could start "The mouse ran up the clock," following the rhyme of "Hickory, Dickory, Dock."

- The book could represent a low-rise apartment building with different families living on each of the four levels. Ask the children to draw and name each family.

★ Helpful hint: Add a personal touch to this book by titling it with the recipient's name on front, e.g., "A present for my mom." Also, try binding each holiday postcard wallet on a separate page in a hard-covered accordion book (see page 52).

House in the forest

1. Follow step 1 of the basic fold-away book. Fold the top panel backwards to the centre. Then, fold the corners diagonally forwards and backwards.

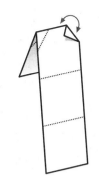

2. Tuck the two folded corners in on themselves and zigzag the pages, as shown.

✏️ USE IT!

- Use the story of Hansel and Gretel as a basis for this project. Ask children to draw the witch's house of candy on the second panel. They can write how Hansel escapes in the remaining panels.

- Who lives in this house? Choose a traditional story that features a house, such as Little Red Riding Hood, The Gingerbread Man or Snow White. The class should draw a house in the style of their chosen story and then list the main characters.

Storyteller's throne

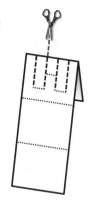

1. Follow step 1 of the basic fold-away book. Fold the top panel backwards to the centre and cut two strips, as shown.

2. Fold the cut sections forwards and backwards. Also fold the centre strip in half backwards and forwards. Unfold the paper fully.

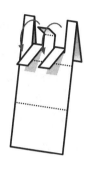

3. As you zigzag the pages into a book, a pop-up chair appears. Magic!

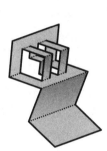

✏️ USE IT!

- A storyteller's throne should look grand, so ask the children to draw swirling patterns on the cushions and precious stones on the arms and back!

"The House Made of Sweets" by Lucy (aged 7). Students folded the book themselves and then drew a house. The stand-up illustration provides a colorful visual reference for the description of the house written beneath it.

8 – Animal books 1

Animals have a special attraction for the young and feature predominantly in stories from all over the world. All the books in this section use the origami book form to make an animal shape. Use the body part for writing.

Make the basic animal book

1. Make the basic zigzag book. Open it out fully to a landscape position and then fold widthways in half. On the folded edge cut along the middle crease as far as the centre.

2. Open the sheet and fold it lengthways in half. Sketch an animal shape on the paper and cut away the unneeded parts.

3. Push the left and right sides of the book inwards to enable the animal shape to stand up.

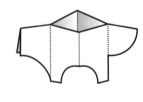

CUTTING MULTIPLES

Follow step 1 above. Cut away a section of paper as shown. Open up the paper fully, fold it lengthways in half, and cut out the front and back sections as you did in step 2.

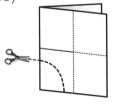

- Ask the children to imagine they are one of Santa Claus's reindeers. What does it feel like to fly across the sky? What happens when they return home after delivering all the presents? Do they give and receive presents too? After writing on the body, suggest that the children cut out antlers and glue them to the reindeer's head.

Raining cats and dogs!

1. Make the basic animal book up to step 2. Open the book out flat.

2. Cut head style *a* for a cat or head style *b* for a dog.

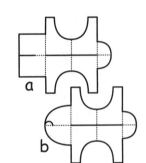

3. Fold the paper lengthways in half. Push the left and right sides of the book inwards to create a standing animal.

Note: If you are making the cat, fold the head panels vertically to the left and right.

⭐ Helpful hint: When cutting the head shape, make sure that you don't cut into the middle panels.

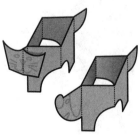

USE IT! ✏️

- Set a task with a title like "Where's Wag the Puppy?" The class should draw Wag and write a narrative such as this:

  Is Wag under the table? No.
  Is Wag behind the TV? No.

  Is Wag …? No.
  Is Wag …? Yes!

- Create a cat or dog character soon to have a birthday. Ask the class to make a birthday card and some paper gifts as birthday presents.

A day at the farm

1. Make the basic cat/dog book to step 2.

2. Push the left and right sides of the book inwards to create a standing animal and fold diagonal ears to make a pig or a cow.

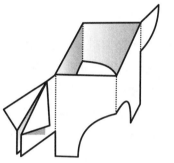

Endangered species

1. Make the basic cat/dog book up to step 1.

2. Fold the paper lengthways in half. Push the left and right sides of the book inwards to create a standing animal.

3. Cut the head to look like a rhinoceros.

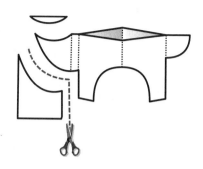

⭐ Helpful hint: Glue the two halves of the animal's head together so that the book is stronger.

USE IT! ✏️

- Some animals, like the rhinoceros, are quite rare. Children could write about protecting wild animals on the sides of the book.

USE IT! ✏️

- Prudence the Pig is about to go off on an adventure away from the farm. Ask the children to write a short narrative about her adventure.

- On a cow version of the book, the children could write about dairy products, such as milk being made into butter and cheese.

"The Lion and the Mouse" by Zanish (aged 7). The student outlined this popular fable on one side of the lion's body. The teacher drew a lion's head on the board to help with the rendering of the artwork.

9 – Animal books 2

You can make tall animals, like prehistoric creatures, or a cat with its tail in the air by changing the folding pattern of the basic origami book. Or, you can make long, narrow creatures, like a crocodile, by using a different, eight-rectangle folding pattern.

Elephant

1. Make the basic animal book up to step 2. Cut an elephant-shaped head complete with trunk.

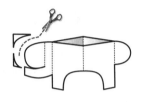

2. Push the left and right sides of the paper inwards to create a standing elephant and fold out the ears.

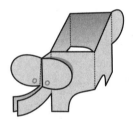

✏️ USE IT!

- Get the class to improvise a story about Herb, an elephant who goes on holiday. What does he take with him on his travels? The children may write what Herb took on one side of the body, and what he did while he was away on the other side.

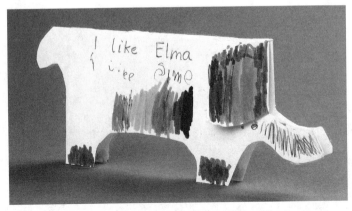

"I like Elma" by Imran (aged 5). The student completed the writing frame "I like …" on the body of this animal book inspired by David McKee's popular elephant character, Elma. The area surrounding the text is decorated with felt-tipped pen.

Long, thin animals

1. Cut a sheet of letter or ledger size paper lengthways in half. Fold the paper into eight equal rectangles and then open it out.

2. Next, fold the paper widthways in half and make a cut on the folded edge as far as the centre.

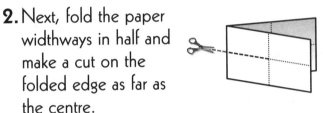

3. Open out the paper again and then fold it lengthways in half. Cut out a long, thin animal shape, such as a crocodile.

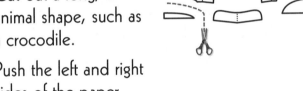

4. Push the left and right sides of the paper inwards to make the crocodile stand up.

✏️ USE IT!

- Children can write the crocodile's name on its body and illustrate the rest as they wish. If you draw the crocodile but do not cut out the shape, you can use the remaining areas to list what the hungry crocodile might eat in a day.

★ Helpful hint: Instead of writing text on an animal's body, children could write dialogue on a speech bubble and glue it onto its mouth.

Dinosaur

1. Fold a sheet of ledger size paper lengthways in half and then unfold it. Fold the paper widthways in half and unfold it again.

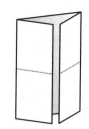

2. Next, with the paper in the portrait position, fold the left and right edges into the centre and unfold.

3. Fold the sheet lengthways in half and make a cut on the horizontal crease, as shown.

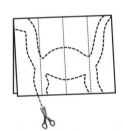

4. Open out the sheet and fold it widthways in half. Push the left and right sides into the centre.

5. Keeping the paper folded, lay it down flat. Draw the shape of a dinosaur and cut it out.

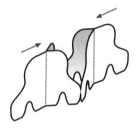

Octopus

1. Make the basic zigzag book and then open it out fully. Fold it widthways in half. Draw a double-octopus shape onto the paper and cut it out as shown.

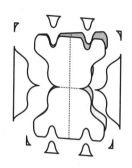

2. Open out the sheet again and fold it lengthways in half.

3. Push the left and right sides all the way into the centre to make a 3D octopus.

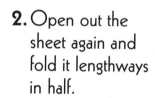

✏️ USE IT!

- The children can write facts about the octopus on its body, e.g., how many tentacles it has, where it lives and what it eats. They can decorate the tentacles with different types of colored paper. Suspend the finished books from the ceiling or from a classroom washing line.

⭐ Helpful hint: Display finished animal books on a background of cut-out paper trees or a seascape.

✏️ USE IT!

- Get the children to write the name of their prehistoric animal on its body. They can then draw in the details of its head and body.

- Using poster-size paper, make a dinosaur for the whole class to decorate with collage.

- Redesign the form as a cat with its tail in the air. Children name the cat and write something about it on the body area.

10 – Pocket folders

Removable objects, such as letters in envelopes, postcards, jigsaw puzzles and games, feature in lots of published children's books. This project integrates a range of writing genres presented as removable objects in a pocket folder.

Make the basic pocket folder

1. Fold the left and right edges of a landscape sheet of letter-size paper into the centre. Unfold them.

2. Fold the sheet lengthways in half. With the folded edge of the paper at the bottom, staple the left and right sides together.

3. Fold the left and right edges of the paper into the centre again – this is the basic folder book.

4. For the book contents, cut some spare paper to make greeting cards, letters, posters and so on. Fit them into the pockets.

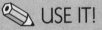

Double pocket folder

1. Fold a sheet of paper widthways in half and unfold. Next, fold the sheet lengthways with the folded edge at the bottom. Leave a gap at the top. This gives you one pocket.

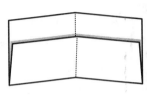

2. Fold the bottom, folded edge up and staple the edges. This gives you another pocket.

3. Again, cut spare paper into pieces to fit into the pockets.

★ Helpful hint: Don't staple the paper too near to the edge or the wallet may weaken and tear.

Pockets with lids

1. Follow step 1 as for the double pocket folder. Then, fold the left and right edges into the centre and unfold. You now have four pockets.

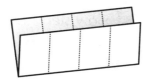

2. Next, fold the back piece of the sheet over the front to make the pocket lids. Unfold. Cut the corners from each of the four pockets and staple the edges of the folder together.

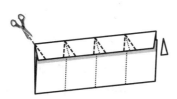

3. Add a title to each of the pockets.

✏ USE IT!

- Ask the children to list everyday tasks, such as reading and math work, on individual pieces of paper and slot them into the pockets in their folders.

- Do a project called "Eating out." Children make one eating-out item per pocket. The items could be a restaurant menu, a list of what they order, the bill, a toothpick or a breath mint.

★ Helpful hint: Set a project to make one big pocket book to contain work from the whole class.

Origami wallet

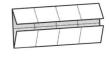

1. Make the basic zigzag book using ledger size paper. Open it out flat in the landscape position. Fold the top and bottom edges into the centre.

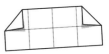

2. Turn the paper over and fold in the corners on the folded edge.

3. Next, fold the left and right edges into the centre.

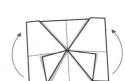

4. Fold back the corners marked *x* diagonally.

5. Fold the paper lengthways in half, tucking the corners behind the flaps you made in step 2.

6. Finally, fold the book widthways in half and you will have a finished origami wallet.

✏ USE IT!

- Discuss with the class what they could put inside the wallet. For example, they could make a bus ticket, a gift token and some play dollar bills.

"Dogum" by Alisha (aged 5). A puppet dog called Dogum owned by the teacher was the basis for a writing project covering half a term. The wallet holds objects like birthday cards, get well cards, presents and letters that students made for the character.

11 – Folded cards

Greeting cards are easy to make and feel special because of the emotional association we have with them. Cards are also an excellent starting point for developing children's sentence-level work.

Make the basic folded card

1. Fold letter size paper in half widthways and then widthways again. Open the paper out fully. Cut a curved-top door, as shown.

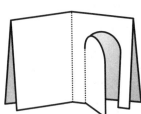

2. Fold the paper in half widthways and widthways again to make the card.

Space rocket card

1. Follow step 1 of how to make the basic folded card, but this time draw and cut out a rocket (or a tree) shape. Take care not to cut the shape out completely.

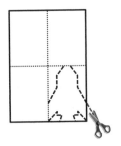

2. Fold the paper in half widthways and then widthways again to make up the card.

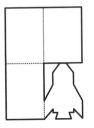

✏ USE IT!

- The children can write a question on the left-hand inside page, such as "Who (or what) is behind the door?" They can illustrate the answer through the door and also write a caption on the back of the door once it's opened.

- Ask the children to design the cover of the card. The title could be "A Surprise!"

✏ USE IT!

- The children can decorate the rocket and draw a space background containing planets, meteorites and stars. Ask them to write what they and their best friend would do on a space mission.

- The class can do a tree house project. After decorating the card, on the inside left page they can start a sentence with "In my tree house there is ..." How will they choose to finish it?

★ Helpful hint: Try using colored papers or thin card for variety.

Pop-up animal card

1. Fold letter size paper in half widthways. Unfold and then fold in half lengthways. Cut a quarter-circle shape on the folded edge, as shown.

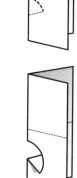

2. Fold the quarter-circle diagonally forward and backward.

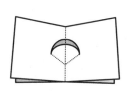

3. Open the paper fully. Fold it widthways in half and in half again to close the card. The pop-up works when the card is opened.

2. Fold the figure forwards and backwards. Unfold.

3. Fold the "neck" part of the figure forwards and backwards. Unfold. Do the same with the "shoulder."

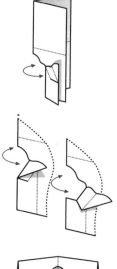

4. Open out the paper fully. Fold it in half widthways and then in half again, pushing the pop-up outwards.

5. Fold the shoulder crease inwards and the neck crease outwards. The jack-in-the-box rises and falls as you open and close the card.

USE IT!

- In an animal-themed project, talk about a rainforest. Children might write "In the rainforest I can see ..." on the front cover of their cards. Inside, they draw a rainforest animal on the pop-up and decorate the background with trees and plants. Ask them to write the animal's name underneath the pop-up.

- Ask the class to make a Lost poster for a cat. How much is the reward? What does the cat look like? How old is he or she?

USE IT!

- Draw a monster on the pop-up, color the box and give the monster a name. Children can make a list of what the monster likes to eat for breakfast or dinner on each side of the pop-up.

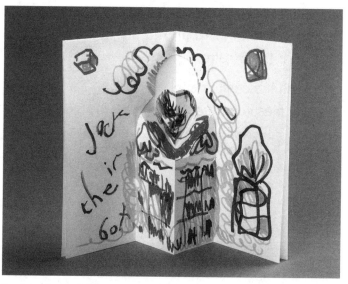

"Jack in the Box" by Jason (aged 5). Jason, a reluctant writer, was inspired to write by this magical pop-up form.

Jack-in-the-box

1. Fold letter size paper in half widthways; unfold and fold it in half lengthways. Draw a half figure shape. Cut the head and shoulders and a small slot on the folded edge as shown.

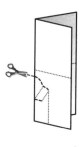

12 – Surprise cards

Pop-up and interlocking greeting cards first appeared in the 1850s. As no glue is required, they are easy to make and can provide a focus for family celebrations and religious festivals.

Make the basic theatre card

1. Fold letter size paper in half lengthways, unfold, and fold in half widthways. Make a cut on the folded edge at a 45° angle as far as the horizontal crease.

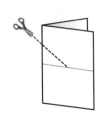

2. Fold the cut panel forwards and backwards. Unfold.

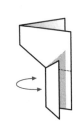

3. Cut the top and bottom of what will be the stage of the theatre. Fold this opening forwards and backwards. Unfold.

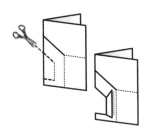

4. Open the paper fully. Fold it lengthways and then widthways in half to close the card and form the theatre.

5. Push the centre panel of the theatre inwards.

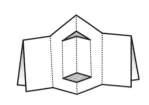

Angled theatre card

1. Make the basic zigzag book, open it out and fold it widthways in half.

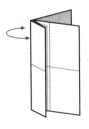

2. Fold the folded edge of the paper into the centre, then fold it backwards to the centre on the other side. Unfold.

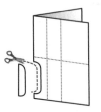

3. Cut a curved window out of the bottom panel.

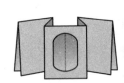

4. Open the sheet out again and fold it in half lengthways. Crease the panels firmly so that the middle window panel projects forward.

★ Helpful hint: Cut out paper figures and glue them behind the theatre window for added 3D effects.

Interlocking theatre card

As this theatre requires careful cutting and assembly, I suggest you make it for the children.

1. Fold letter size paper in half lengthways; unfold. Fold in half widthways and unfold. Then fold it into three equal sections and unfold.

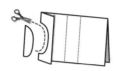

2. Fold the left edge of the paper to the first crease and cut a curved window. Unfold. Repeat this for the right edge.

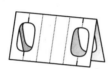

3. Cut slots above and below the windows, as shown in the diagram on the right.

4. Bring the sides of the card together and interlock the slots to make the theatre.

USE IT!

- Children draw a festive party scene through the theatre window and write an invitation to the party on the outer frame. They can decorate the card with seasonal or party objects, like balloons, crackers and presents.

"Father Christmas Coming Down the Chimney" by Faheem (aged 6). After discussing the character, the teacher wrote key words on the board. Faheem composed her own sentence chosen from those words.

Display theatres

Again, due to their complexity, make these theatres for children.

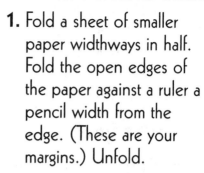

1. Fold a sheet of smaller paper widthways in half. Fold the open edges of the paper against a ruler a pencil width from the edge. (These are your margins.) Unfold.

2. Fold the folded edge of the paper as far as the crease you made in step 1.

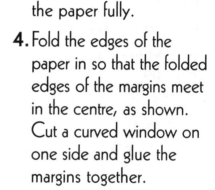

3. Cut as shown and unfold the paper fully.

4. Fold the edges of the paper in so that the folded edges of the margins meet in the centre, as shown. Cut a curved window on one side and glue the margins together.

5. Use the glued margins to join several identical display theatres together.

★ Helpful hint: Make the theatres from black paper and decorate with collage for extra visual impact.

USE IT!

- Join these charming theatres together for a whole class display. Explore different presentation methods.

- Introduce the theme of a garden show.

Children can draw a garden (or an individual flower) through the window opening of the theatre and write a caption on the base: "In spring …"

13 – Theatre books

Children's toy theatres first appeared in the nineteenth century and have retained their popularity ever since. As these theatres require cutting through more than one layer of paper, I recommend you make them for the class.

Make the basic theatre book

1. Make a basic zigzag book from ledger size paper and open it out fully. Fold in half lengthways and widthways. Cut the top and bottom of a flap on the left folded edge.

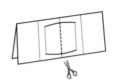

2. Unfold the paper widthways and cut up the centre of the flap to make double doors.

3. Fold back the sides of the paper and slot the left edge into the right one to make an equilateral triangle.

4. Open the doors.

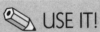

Theatre with drop panels

1. Make a basic zigzag book from ledger size paper and open it out fully. Fold it lengthways and then widthways in half. Cut a right angle on the folded edge.

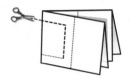

2. Fold the flap forwards and back up again.

3. Unfold the paper widthways and cut up the centre of the flap to make two panels.

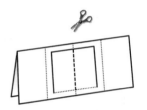

4. Make up the paper into a theatre as before and pull the flaps down to finish.

★ Helpful hint: Experiment with making theatres from decorative paper or wrapping paper.

Theatre with pointed panels

1. Make a basic zigzag book from ledger size paper and open it out fully. Fold it lengthways and widthways in half and then make two cuts as shown.

2. Unfold the paper once and make another cut up the middle creases of the flaps.

3. Make into a theatre as before and open out all the flaps.

✏️ USE IT!

- Make a surprise theatre. Open the pointed flaps to reveal a surprise drawn on the inside, e.g., a bouquet for Mother's Day.

- Read the story "The Snow Queen" by Hans Christian Andersen. Ask the class to draw the queen's palace through the opening. The pointed panels can represent icicles. They can write something about the Snow Queen on the back, such as what sort of person she was.

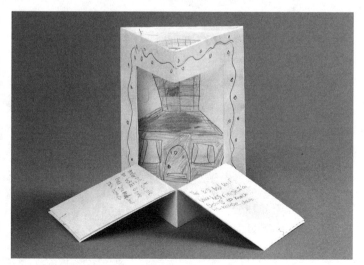

"The Three Little Pigs Play" by Halima (aged 7). The teacher provided a drafting sheet with character headings. The writing is presented on the drop-down panels of the theatre. The background panel shows the brick house. The final stage was to decorate the theatre frame.

Model theatre

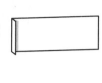

1. Cut a sheet of ledger size paper lengthways in half to make two strips. Take one of the strips and fold a small margin on the left edge.

2. Fold the right edge of the paper over to the left, folded edge. Unfold and turn over. Fold the left folded edge and right edge into the centre. Unfold.

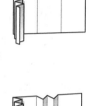

3. Fold the left folded edge to the first crease. Fold the newly formed folded edge to the first crease. Unfold. Use the folds you have made to zigzag this panel, as shown. Repeat with panel 3.

4. Fold panel 2 widthways in half and cut out a curved window. Unfold.

5. Glue the right edge to the left margin and re-crease the sides into zigzags.

6. Make an artwork panel to fit the back of the theatre.

✏️ USE IT!

- Use for a lesson on other cultures. An Aboriginal creation myth tells how light made everything come alive – rivers, plants, birds. Children can draw this scene on a backdrop panel and glue it into the theatre. In a separate zigzag book, they can make a list of the things that grew once light came to the world.

★ Helpful hint: Display the theatres three-dimensionally, but store them flat.

14 – Pop-up theatres

Pop-ups have an endless fascination for children and so they make good stimuli for writing projects. These "ninety-degree" theatres are easy to make and can be joined together to make a pop-up book if desired.

Make the basic pop-up theatre

1. Cut a sheet of letter size paper lengthways in half to make two strips. Take one strip and, in the portrait position, fold over a crease on the top edge.

2. Next, fold the top folded edge down to the bottom edge and unfold.

3. Fold the top folded edge down again but this time by 2 cm (about ¾ in.). Fold the bottom edge up to touch the creased edge. Unfold.

4. Draw and cut out a curved stage opening, as shown.

5. Turn the paper upside down. Draw your scene on back bottom panel.

6. Fold the top down and glue it to the flap on the base.

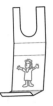

7. Fold the second strip widthways in half to form a back and base. Glue the stage into it.

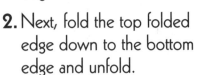 USE IT!

- Ask the students to draw a child waving in welcome on the theatre backdrop. They then glue the theatre to the base and write "Welcome to our school ..." in the foreground area.

Car, shop or house

1. Make the basic pop-up theatre as far as step 4, but this time draw and cut out a house, store or car shape instead of the stage opening.

2. Complete the background artwork and then follow steps 6 and 7 as before.

3. Flatten the theatre and draw in the detail of the car, store or house, then glue it onto the base.

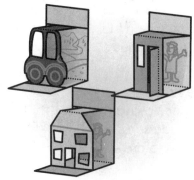

★ Helpful hint: Don't glue the theatre until all the inside artwork has been completed.

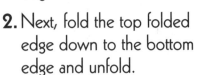 USE IT!

- After drawing a car, children write a first person description of where the driver is going. They could make it a special journey.

- "What does my store sell?" Ask the children to draw a store and list the things it sells on the front panel.

- Students draw a house on the theatre and describe who lives there, including pets, on the front panel.

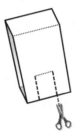

"The Magic Car" by Hassan (aged 5). The teacher drew the car template, photocopied it for the class and then, with the help of a teaching assistant, cut and folded it down to the pop-up form, ready for use. Students did the gluing.

Theatre with pop-up figure

1. Make the basic pop-up theatre, including the background artwork, but don't glue it to the base yet. Instead, make two small parallel cuts on the back of the theatre to make a flap.

2. Fold the flap forwards and backwards. Unfold. This will form a small pop-up cube.

3. Carefully raise the pop-up cube on the inside of the theatre.

4. Glue an archway-shaped figure panel onto the pop-up cube and complete the rest of theatre as before.

★ Helpful hint: Don't cut the arch opening too near to the edge of the paper.

✏️ **USE IT!**

- Every student chooses someone he or she admires. Ask them to draw this person and a suitable background, e.g., a hockey player and an arena. Then they can write a diary entry for that person.

- Children make a figure of Tom Thumb and write one advantage and one disadvantage of being tiny.

Pop-up theatre book

Make three complete pop-up theatres. Glue them together and then put them in a fold-around cover.

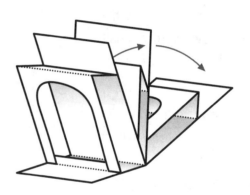

✏️ **USE IT!**

- Draw the story of Jack and the Beanstalk on the backdrops of three theatres and/or make pop-up figures as described for the "Theatre with pop-up figure." The theatre sequence could be as follows:

1. Jack climbs up the beanstalk.
2. Jack goes inside the castle and sees the giant.
3. Jack comes down the beanstalk with the gold.

The children can write about each episode on the front panel of each theatre. Discussion points: How does the story start? What happens when Jack gets to the top of the beanstalk? What happens at the end of the story?

15 – Backdrop pop-ups

This style of paper engineering is commonly found in published pop-up books so examples should be quite easy to find. One of the advantages of this backdrop form is that it leaves almost the whole of the base available for children's writing.

Make the basic backdrop pop-up

1. Fold letter size paper in half widthways to form a base and put it on one side. Fold another sheet of same-size paper in half widthways and cut it into two strips along the crease. Take one of the two pieces and fold it in half lengthways. Cut a small triangle from the bottom corner of the folded edge.

2. Make a margin by folding the bottom edge forwards and backwards as far as the top of the triangle cut. Unfold.

3. Draw and cut out a rocket shape, as shown.

4. After you've completed the writing and drawing (see Use It!), glue both sides of the margin to the base reserved in step 1. Line up the cut-off triangle with the crease in the middle of the base.

5. Fold the base down over the pop-up. Allow the glue to dry completely before use.

★ Helpful hint: Always glue the margins flat. Don't fold them into a right angle and then glue them.

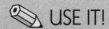 USE IT!

- Decorate the pop-up rocket with faces looking out of the windows. Children can use the left-hand side of the base to make the astronaut's checklist for a journey into space. They can use the right-hand side for a first-person description of taking off. "I pressed the button and …"

Tropical island

1. Complete steps 1 and 2 of the basic backdrop pop-up. Draw and cut out a palm tree shape instead of a rocket.

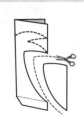

2. Next, complete step 4 of the basic backdrop pop-up.

3. Take the discarded strip of paper and cut it lengthways in half. Fold one piece widthways in half — and save the other piece for another project. Cut a triangle from the bottom of the folded edge. Follow step 2 of the basic backdrop pop-up.

4. Draw and cut a simple beach scene from the strip, shaping the top of the strip for interest.

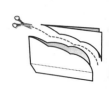

5. Glue the strip's margin to the base. Line up the cut-off triangle with the base's middle crease.

6. Allow the glue to dry completely before use.

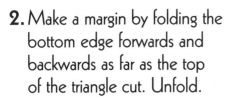

- Ask the class to decorate the tree and island pop-ups. Write on the base how you would try to escape if you were marooned on an island.

- The pop-up tropical island is an advertisement in a travel brochure. Write some text making it sound like a good place to go on holiday.

Backdrop with pop-up figures

1. Make the basic pop-up base. Cut another piece of paper the same size as the base in half widthways. Fold one of these cut pieces in half widthways. Cut a triangle from the bottom edge and crease a margin forwards and backwards at the top of the triangle. Unfold.

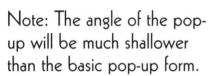

2. Draw a park or a shop on the paper.

3. Glue both sides of the margin to the base. Line up the cut-off triangle with the middle crease at point *a*. Allow the glue to dry.

   Note: The angle of the pop-up will be much shallower than the basic pop-up form.

4. To make a pop-up figure, take the other piece of paper and cut a small strip from one of its short edges; then, crease a margin.

5. Glue the margin to the other end of the paper. Fold the paper in half and then open it out to form a square-shaped ring.

6. Glue the square ring to the pop-up and the base.

7. Make a figure panel and glue it to the square ring. Make other pop-up figure panels like this and attach them in the same way.

8. Sometimes pop-ups will drop forward. To counteract this, make a small mountain crease on the valley crease in the base near the front of the pop-up.

⭐ Helpful hint: The thicker the paper you use, the stronger the glue will need to be.

- Children make a backdrop of trees and pop-up figures playing games for a park scene. They write captions to describe the games being played.

- Ask the class to draw a storefront and make a pop-up girl and a boy shopper. Write a shopping list, the cost of each item and the grand total.

"I went to the park …" by Lynette (aged 4). The teacher has word-processed Lynette's oral narrative and attached it to the base. Lynette felt pride in seeing herself in print, which was an effective writing stimulus.

16 – Tower pop-ups

This is another popular pop-up engineering technique found in published children's books. I call it "tower" because the pop-up rises like one. As the pop-up sits in the middle of the base, writing projects can be added around it.

Make the basic tower pop-up

1. Fold a sheet of letter size paper in half widthways to form a base. Cut another same-size sheet in half lengthways. Crease a margin on the left edge of one of the pieces of paper.

2. Fold and glue the right edge of the paper to the margin.

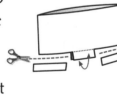

3. Measure 1cm (3/8 in.) from the bottom edge of the paper and cut to make two tabs in the centre. Fold the tabs forwards and backwards. Unfold. Complete all the artwork at this stage before proceeding to step 4.

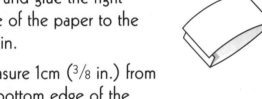

4. Apply glue to both sides of the tabs. Stick one tab to the left side of the base. Allow 2 cm (3/4 in.) between the crease in the base and the tab. Close the base so it sticks to the other tab, allow the glue to dry and then open it again.

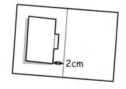

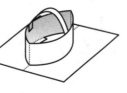

5. Glue in a handle cut from a spare piece of paper.

There was an old woman ...

The rhyme "There was an old woman who lived in a shoe" is a popular theme for classroom projects.

1. Make the basic pop-up base. Cut another sheet of letter size paper widthways in half . Crease a margin on the left edge. Fold and glue the right edge of the paper to the margin. Cut out two tabs as with the basic tower pop-up.

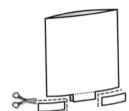

2. Cut out two pieces to leave the shape of a shoe, as shown.

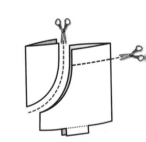

3. Glue the shoe to the base, as for the basic tower pop-up. If the pop-up tends to close, make a small mountain crease on the valley crease in the base, near the front of the pop-up.

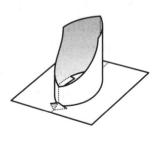

★ Helpful hint: Ensure that nothing protrudes outside the closed pop-up base.

Bag or box

1. Make the basic tower pop-up up to step 3. Fold the left and right edges 2 cm (3/4 in.) forwards and backwards to make side flaps. Unfold.

2. Fold the side flaps inwards.

3. Measure 2 cm (3/4 in.) from the base crease to the front of the pop-up and glue down the tabs. Allow to dry before using.

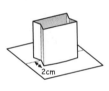

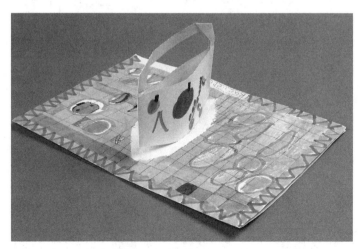

"Picnic Hamper" by Rachel and Tom (aged 6). One student drew and cut out food to put into the picnic hamper. The other student drew the picnic spread on the base. They worked together to write a list of the contents of the hamper on the back.

Noah's ark

1. Use large, thick paper for this project. Complete steps 1 to 3 of the basic tower pop-up. Draw and cut out an ark shape.

2. Fold the roof in half forwards and backwards. Unfold.

3. At the top of the roof, fold a narrow margin forwards and backwards. Unfold.

4. Fold the roof margin edges inwards and glue them together.

5. Crease triangular-shaped margins on the side edges of the ark and fold them forwards and backwards.

6. Fold these edge margins inwards. Glue the ark to the base as for the bag or box form, but allow a slightly wider gap between the bottom of the ark and the crease in the base.

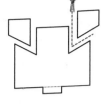

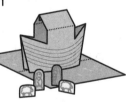

17 – Puzzle books

Flexagons are intriguing for adults and children alike. Make the basic form first and then demonstrate the final gluing and the manipulation of the flexagon to the whole class. Let individual children experience the opening process themselves before they make their own puzzle books.

Make the basic flexagon

1. Fold a sheet of letter size paper lengthways in half and then in half again. Unfold and fold widthways in half and then in half again. Unfold and remove the bottom four panels.

2. Number the squares, as above, and cut around three sides of the centre panels.

3. Turn the paper over and number the panels, as shown in the second diagram.

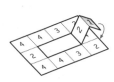

4. Turn over. Fold the centre panels over the right edge.

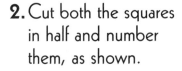

5. Fold the left edge of the paper inwards once and then fold it in again.

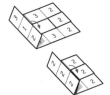

6. Turn the sheet over and join the middle panels with a small strip of glued paper

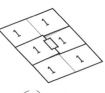

7. To use the flexagon, keep folding until you can see all the panels marked 2, then again to 3, and so on.

★ Helpful hint: When gluing sections together, make sure that the glue doesn't spread to other parts; otherwise, it may stop the book from opening easily.

42

Flexagon-again!

1. Cut identical squares from two pieces of ledger or letter size paper. Take one square and fold the left and right edges into the centre. Unfold and repeat for the other square.

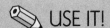

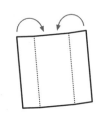

2. Cut both the squares in half and number them, as shown.

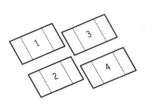

3. Glue the corners of panels 3 and 4 to panels 1 and 2.

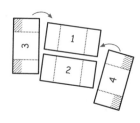

4. Follow the opening diagrams to work the flexagon.

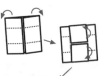

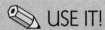

★ Helpful hint: Open the folds carefully — it's easy to tear them while you get the hang of how the book works.

Jacob's ladder

This book — based on an ancient child's toy from China — is mystifying and magical. Let children watch you assemble it first.

1. Use a basic 8-panel book made from large paper. Open it out and remove the top middle panels.

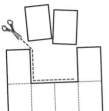

2. Fold the paper in half widthways. Make four equal cuts on the folded edge to form strips. Unfold.

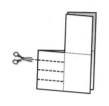

3. Fold down the top panels. Slot one of the panels through the strips on page 2 in an over/under weaving-style pattern. Do the same with the second panel on page 3, but start by going UNDER the strip first.

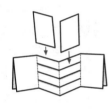

4. Fold into a zigzag so that the middle pages protrude forward. Find the hidden gap between pages 2 and 3 with your thumbs and open them out to reveal two more pages! Close the pages to return to the basic zigzag book.

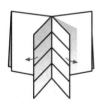

✏️ USE IT!

- As a display feature, make a large Jacob's ladder book and glue individual students' work on the strips. A suggested writing frame could be a project entitled "My Body Book." The frame could begin "I've got fingers (toes, eyes, ...)"

Puzzle wallet

Children find this wallet a mystery, as it opens from both sides.

1. Use a basic zigzag book made from ledger size paper. Fold it in half and make three equal cuts on the folded edge to form strips.

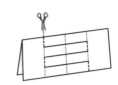

2. Unfold the book once and make four cuts, as shown. You will now have two pieces of paper: *a* and *b*.

3. Glue the two open strips together on both of the pieces.

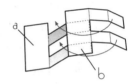

4. Zigzag the strips of piece *a* and glue their ends behind panel *b*.

5. Fold the *b* strips over to the left and under piece *a*.

6. Fold piece *b* under piece *a*.

7. Fold the end strips of piece *b* over piece *a* and glue them. Open the wallet. Make small panels to slot into the wallet.

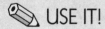

✏️ USE IT!

- Students draw their favorite photographic scenes (my holiday, my mom, my best friend, our visit to the park) on at least two pieces of paper. Talk about captions and ask students to include one under each scene before placing them inside the wallet.

43

18 – Invisible-join books

In the first three join books, the joining staple is hidden from view, so see if children can work out how they are made. The fourth book joins pages without attachments of any kind — quite a mystery and lots of fun!

Make the basic invisible-join book

1. Fold two pieces of letter size paper separately in half lengthways and widthways. Unfold.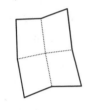

2. Put the sheets together in the portrait position and staple through the bottom vertical crease using a long-arm stapler.

3. Drop the top half of the front page down forwards and the top half of the back page down backwards.

4. Fold the centre crease to complete book.

   Note: A long-arm stapler is needed.

✏️ USE IT!

- Set the class a color book project. They can title the book: "My Color Book." Ask them to use spread 1 for red objects, spread 2 for yellow and spread 3 for blue. Children list and draw things that are associated with those colors, such as a red apple and a yellow chick.

Stapled book with cover

1. Fold two pieces of letter size paper separately in half lengthways and widthways. Unfold. Repeat to another piece of paper, preferably colored, to form the book cover. Fold one of the white sheets in half widthways and lay it on the bottom half of the colored piece.

2. Place the other open white piece of paper on top. Hold firmly together and staple all the pages through the bottom half of the vertical crease using a long-arm stapler.

3. Fold the front sheet forwards and the colored sheet backwards.

4. Fold the centre crease to close book.

✏️ USE IT!

- Children draw and caption favorite playground games on each spread. Discuss issues such as how to improve the playground or what safety rules to follow for playing games.

- On each page students can write a way of making their school a happy place, such as sharing or taking turns, and make a drawing to go with it.

Side-stapled book

1. For the pages: Place six folded sheets of paper together with all the folded edges on one side and the open edges on the other. As the first and last sheets are the cover, use colored paper for them. Staple all the sheets together near the edge of the open edges. You can add extra pages if required before stapling, but don't add too many because standard staples can only join so many sheets together.

2. For the spine decoration: Cut a strip of colored paper the height of pages and about 4 cm (1 ½ in.) wide. Fold the strip lengthways in half.

3. Decorate the strip with colored pens before gluing it over the stapled edge.

✏ USE IT!

- Ask the class to write a poem on a folded sheet of paper (with the fold on the right-hand side). The theme could be a favorite toy they had when they were younger. Where is it now? Collate the pages and make them into a book for each table or group.

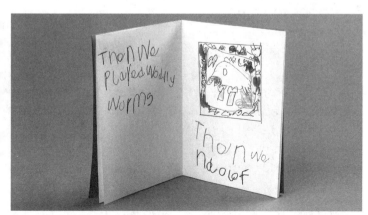

"Our Visit to Beaulieu Park" by Cerys (aged 5). A school visit was discussed and then described in words and pictures in this record book. Each page describes a different part of the day.

★ Helpful hint: Leave a generous margin on the spine side of all pages before writing or drawing because this part of the page is hidden inside the stapled edge. The first few words will be lost if the margin is too small.

Locked-pages book

See if the children can work out the clever construction of this book.

1. Fold two sheets of letter size paper lengthways and widthways. Unfold. Cut the paper widthways in half. Place two sheets together and make a cut down the centre crease ⅓ from the top of the book and another one ⅓ up the crease from the bottom of the book.

2. Place the other two sheets together. Make a ⅓ cut in the centre of the crease.

3. Curve one side of the first two sheets and slot it through the cutting "hole" of the second two sheets.

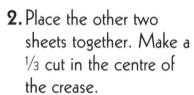
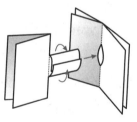

4. Open out the curved pages on the other side of the slot to complete the book.

✏ USE IT!

- Children write on the cover: "My Wish Book by ..." They complete a writing frame at the bottom of each page as follows: "I wish that I could ..." They then draw a picture above.

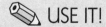

45

19 – Books with covers

These folded books look like real books because they have a spine and are beautiful, aesthetic objects for children to treasure. Experiment with making these books in different sizes.

Make the basic book with a cover

1. Open the basic zigzag book and fold it widthways in half. On the folded edge, make a cut on the horizontal crease.

2. Open out the book and make a cut in the middle of the two vertical creases.

3. Fold the top half of the sheet forward and open out the middle pages.

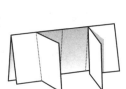

4. Fold the paper widthways in half so that the back middle pages touch. Fold the first and last panels forward against the other panels to close the book.

5. For the spine, cut a strip of colored paper the height of the book and 4 cm (1 ½ in.) wide. Fold it in half lengthways, unfold and glue it over the book spine.

Book with a detachable cover

1. For the pages, use the basic zigzag book made from letter size paper. Open the book and make a cut on the horizontal crease.

2. Fold the top half of the paper over the bottom half and zigzag the pages on either side of the middle panels.

3. For the cover, use colored paper. Fold the left edge almost all the way over the right edge — leave a gap of up to 2 cm (³/₄ in.). Repeat with the other side. You now have a spine.

4. Fold the left edge inwards to within about 1 cm (³/₈ in.) of the spine to make a pocket. Repeat on the other side.

5. Slot the first page of the book into the left pocket of the cover. Repeat on the other side and close the book to finish.

Flower book

1. Make a basic book with a detachable cover, as on page 46. Open the cover and fold the second panel on the right vertically in half. Cut as shown.

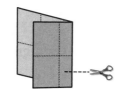

2. Open out the sheet and cut up and down from the cut you have just made to make a cross. This will form the flower petals.

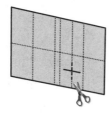

3. Drop the top half of the paper down behind the bottom half. Open the petals.

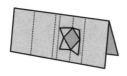

4. Fold the outer panels inwards and insert the pages, as before.

★ Helpful hint: Don't forget to write the title of the book on the spine.

USE IT!

- The class can make a collection of leaves or garden flowers and press them into the book, labelling each one as they go.

- How flowers grow: Ask children to use the first page of the book as the title page and the remaining five pages for illustrating a seed, bulb, stalk, petals and flower head.

- Children write a story called "The Sad Flower." Why is it sad and how does it become happy again?

A forward and backward book

This eighteenth-century technique joins two books together by attaching the second book to the back cover of the first.

1. For the pages, make two sets of pages as for a "Book with a detachable cover."

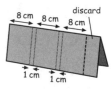

2. For the cover, fold colored paper lengthways in half. From the left edge of the paper mark points 8 cm (3 in.) along, then 1 cm (3/8 in.), then 8 cm, then 1 cm and finally another 8 cm. Discard the remaining paper.

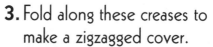

3. Fold along these creases to make a zigzagged cover.

4. Glue the first set of pages into front cover section and the second set into the back one.

USE IT!

- For a seasonal project, children can use the first book to show what they like about summer; the second, for what they like about winter.

- The first book can be used for a series of questions and the second one for the answers. Title this

"My Family" by Siân (aged 4). Siân made this celebration book as a gift for her family.

20 – Sewn books

Making books by sewing pages together goes back to antiquity and so introduces children to the book as a cultural archetype. In the hard-covered form, these books are excellent for presenting and protecting whole-class projects.

Make the basic sewn book with a paper cover

1. One by one, fold in half and then open sheets of high-quality letter size paper. Place the sheets together. Add another, thicker, folded sheet as the cover. Hold the open pages and the cover tightly together using bulldog clips. Using a bookbinder's awl or the point of a pair of compasses, make three evenly spaced holes though the centre fold.

2. Take a length of strong thread four times the height of the pages and thread it onto a strong needle. Starting on the inside of the pages, sew through the middle hole. Leave a "tail" at the front for tying a knot and secure it under the bulldog clip. Keep the thread tight, but not so tight as to bow the pages.

3. Sew through the top hole and then through the middle hole again.

4. Sew through the bottom hole.

5. Remove the needle from the thread, and the tail from the clip. Tie a knot tightly over the middle hole and neatly trim the ends of the thread.

★ Helpful hint: Ensure that the knot is tight; otherwise the pages will be loose.

✏ USE IT!

- Use this book for something special like a recount of a visit to a farm or an original story created by the student. Plan how many pages you need in advance. A set of sewn pages is called a section. Do not sew more than ten sheets of folded paper together into a single section.

Make the basic sewn book with a hard cover

1. For the pages, follow the same instructions as for paper-covered sewn books but don't add a sheet for the cover. If using larger paper make five equally spaced holes on the centre crease with the top and bottom ones nearer to the edge. The length of thread needs to be twice the height of the book, plus enough to tie a knot. Start the sewing on the outside, not the inside, and sew in loops.

2. For the front cover, lay the folded pages on a piece of board. Mark a 0.5 cm (³/₁₆ in.) margin at the top and bottom, but no margins on the left- and right-hand sides. Cut it out and make a duplicate for the back cover.

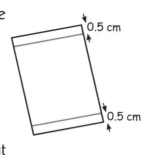

0.5 cm

0.5 cm

3. The width of the spine is determined by the number of pages in the book and by the mounted work on the pages. With the book pages loosely closed, measure the thickness. Add a bit more to this to determine how wide the spine should be. Don't make the spine less than a pencil width. Lightly glue the centre of the covers and the spine to good-quality paper. Allow a 2 cm (³/₄ in.) margin around the edges and about 0.5 cm between the covers and the spine (for larger books, allow 1 cm).

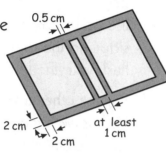

0.5 cm

2 cm

2 cm

at least 1 cm

4. Glue the cover corners diagonally over the boards.

5. When the glue is dry, fold the four margins tightly over the boards. Unfold. Apply glue to the edges of the left- and right-hand side margins. Leave until they feel tacky and then press down. Then do the same to the top and bottom margins.

6. Turn to the back of the pages; glue the edges and the spine. Lay the pages in position on the cover, lining up the middle crease of the pages with the centre of the

spine, and ensuring that the top, bottom and right margins are all equal.

7. Glue down the back of the first page in the same way.

8. Allow the glue to dry. Before closing the book, lightly run your finger down the gap between the cover board and the spine. Doing so will help stop the page glued onto the cover from lifting off, which is what happens if you close the book with the glue still wet.

★ Helpful hint: Put a piece of paper between your hand and the glued area when smoothing down. This will help keep the book clean.

✎ USE IT!

- Knowing how to produce bound books enables you and your class to develop books with a longer life span. They can become reference books on themes that the class explores, with each child contributing one page. They can also showcase children's artwork. To create pages, remember to fold larger sheets, such as chart paper, in half. Work out the number of pages needed and then add two more for gluing into the cover.

"Under the Sea" by a Kindergarten class. A photographic record of the stages in making a sea-life project is compiled in this bound book.

21 – Side-bound books

Side binding is a beautiful technique perfected by the Japanese. The sewing is visible on the outside of the cover and so the sewing pattern is an integral part of the book's design.

Make the basic side-bound book

1. The pages can be of any size. Either fold the pages in half and lay one on top of the other with the folded edges on the left and the open edges on the right, or place the sheets together unfolded.

2. To make the cover, lay one page on a piece of board. Measure a 0.5 cm (3/16 in.) margin on all sides. Cut it out and then make another piece the same size.

3. Cut a 2 cm (3/4 in.) strip from the left edge of one piece of board (or wider for larger books). Next, remove (but keep) a 1 cm (3/8 in.) strip from the left edge of the large remaining piece.

4. Glue the larger strip to the cover material allowing for a 2 cm (3/4 in.) margin on the left and the bottom. Lay as a guide the 1 cm (3/8 in.) strip next to it and glue the large piece next to that. Remove the smaller strip.

5. Trim margins, as shown.

6. Glue down the corners and edges as for hard-covered books (see page 49).

7. Cut some thin, colored paper slightly smaller than the cover. Glue the edges and use it to line the inside. Repeat all the above steps to the duplicate piece of card.

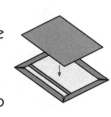

8. Lay the back cover face down with the 2 cm (3/4 in.) margin on the left. Lay the pages on the back cover with the open edges on the right side and the folded edges flush with the left edge.

9. Lay the other cover on top face up with the margin on the left. Holding the book tightly, lay pieces of paper over the top edge to protect the covers and secure them with large bulldog clips at the top and bottom.

Making holes and sewing

Make four equally spaced holes with a bookbinder's awl through the gap between the cover boards. Check that a needle will fit easily through the holes.

Measure a length of thread equal to twice the height of the book. Add on enough thread to go over the spine four times, and to tie a knot and make a hanging loop at the end. If you're using thin thread, sew a double thickness and double all the lengths above.

★ Helpful hint: For more colorful effects, combine two or more strands of contrasting colored thread.

Sewing pattern

1. Sew through the front top hole. Tuck at least a 10 cm (4 in.) tail under clip. From the back, go over the spine and through the top hole a second time.

2. Go down to hole 2, through to the front, over the spine and through hole 2 again.

3. Go down to the front of hole 3, go through to the back, over the spine and through hole 3 again.

4. Go down to hole 4, through to the front, over the spine and through hole 4 again to the front.

5. Go under the bottom of the book and through hole 4 a third time.

6. Go up to hole 3 and through to the back.

7. Go up to hole 2 and through to the front.

8. Go up to the top hole and through to the back.

9. Release the tail from the clip on the front of the book. Remove the needle and bring the thread end to the front of the book. Tie a knot over the top of the front hole. Tie a knot at the end of the thread to make a hanging loop. Remove the clips. Lightly run a finger down the grooves on the covers before opening.

✏️ USE IT!

- These books are excellent for binding single, large sheets of children's work or thematic mounted work. You simply line up the pages and sew them along the edge.

"Easter" by a Kindergarten class. This book is a compilation of marbled Easter eggs made by students and mounted on single sheets of paper before being sewn into the book.

22 – Accordion books

Book pages that open in a zigzag fashion originated in ancient China. No stitching is required and you can add extra pages after binding.

Make the basic accordion book

1. Make the basic zigzag book with large size paper. Open out the book fully and, in the landscape position, fold the left and right edges into the centre. Make two cuts on either side of the folded edges, as shown, and fold the panels forwards and backwards. Unfold.

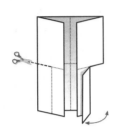

2. Open the sheet and fold it lengthways in half. Zigzag the pages, as shown. Make three more books like this.

3. Join them up by gluing the last and first pages together.

★ Helpful hint: Use a weight to keep it still while the glue dries.

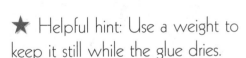

✏ USE IT!

- This book is useful if you are uncertain about how many pages you need to bind a class project. You can open the book and display it panoramically. It serves whole-class theme work well, e.g., the story of a letter. Each child draws and captions one sequence on a sheet of paper:
1. Writing a letter,
2. Putting the letter in an envelope,
3. Addressing the envelope, and so on until the second last page, which shows the mail carrier delivering the letter. The final page shows the recipient reading it.

Mounting children's work

Each piece of paper that you use should be letter size, folded into four zigzag panels and finally glued onto the accordion book base.

Open binding cover

Make two card covers slightly larger than your pages and glue them separately to the backs of the first and last pages.

Hard-covered accordion book

1. Use the same covers as for an open binding cover but add a card spine. To house a whole class's work this spine should be about 4 cm (1 ½ in.) wide. Lightly glue the centre of the boards to good-quality paper, allowing 2 cm ($^3/_4$ in.) margins on the edges and 0.5 cm ($^3/_{16}$ in.) between the spine and the covers. Cut the corners off, leaving a small distance between the corner of the board and the edge of the paper.

2. Glue the side margins to the boards. Glue down the top and bottom margins.

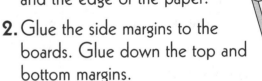

3. For the cover lining, cut paper to fit the inside back cover and spine and extend a pencil width over the inside front cover. Glue the edges and attach.

4. To make the pages, cut large size paper in half lengthways and zigzag the two strips to four-fold

size. Join the sections together with tape. Repeat until you have enough sections.

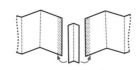

5. Glue the back edges of the first page and attach them to the inside of the front cover. Before closing the book, gently run a finger down the gap between the covers and the spine.

Buckram spine and corners cover

To strengthen hard-covered books, use bookbinder's cloth tape to make the spine and reinforce the corners. This is particularly beneficial to frequently handled books.

1. Cover the front and back cover boards separately using the techniques described on page 52.

2. Cut a spine from buckram 4 cm (1 ½ in.) higher than the cover boards and wide enough to cover the spine width, the gaps between the spine and 2 cm (³/₄ in.) of the cover edges. Apply glue to the back of the buckram and attach the spine board to the centre. Attach the cover boards to the strip, remembering to leave a gap between the cover and the spine.

3. Glue the buckram strip over the spine. Follow the remaining steps as above to complete the book.

4. For the corners, cut four buckram squares about 6 cm (2 ¼ in.) square. (You will need a larger square for larger books). Fold the squares in half diagonally in both directions, and then remove one of the triangles as shown.

5. Glue the squares onto the outside and inside corners of the cover. You can do this before or after you attach the pages.

★ Helpful hint: As an alternative to buckram, the stiffened cloth used in bookbinding, you can use strong cotton fabric.

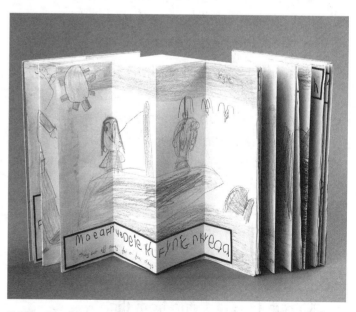

"Michael and Emma are going to France" by John (aged 5). This book tells the story of two children going on holiday in sequenced pictures drawn on separate sheets of paper. After completing the illustrations, the teacher assisted the student in providing a page-by-page narrative on strips of paper. These strips were glued to the bottom of each of the relevant pages. The final stage was to assemble the pages into the accordion book form shown here.

23 – Stories in boxes

We associate decorative boxes with something special hiding inside — so make the books inside these boxes special too.

Make the basic story box

1. For the box lid, make the largest square possible from letter size paper.

2. Fold all the corners into the centre and unfold. Fold all the corners to the first sets of creases you've made. Unfold. Fold all the corners again, as shown. Unfold.

3. Make four cuts — these are flaps (see step 5).

4. Fold the top left and bottom right corners in as far as the first crease. Fold them in again as far as the next crease.

5. Raise the sides and fold the flaps you made in step 3 inwards. Fold up the remaining two corners and tuck in the flaps. For the box base, remove about 0.5 cm (3/16 in.) from one long and one short edge of the paper. Assemble as for the lid.

6. For the pages, remove about 0.5 cm (3/16 in.) strip from the short edge of letter size paper. Fold the sheet widthways in half and half again. Cut it into three equal horizontal strips, and zigzag them with tape. Fit the pages into the box, as shown, and add the lid.

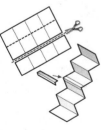
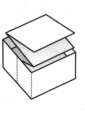

✏ USE IT!

- Improvise a story with the class about a magic box. What's inside? Does it have special powers? What can it do?

- Lay out the strips vertically. Ask the children to start writing on the bottom panel and add an illustration above it. They continue in the same way on the other two strips. Join all the zigzags together using tape on the rear side. House the class collection of stories in a story box.

Matchbox story

Start collecting empty matchboxes several months before you do this project. Photocopy the book template on page 63. Reserve the first and last pages to tuck into the cover and the first right-hand side page as a title page so that there are six spreads for the story.

1. Cut out the pages panel and fold it in half with the dotted lines on the outside. Unfold.

2. Fold the left and right edges into the centre with the dotted lines on the inside. Unfold.

3. Turn the paper around and repeat. Cut the dashed lines as marked on the template and zigzag all the pages in an "over, under" pattern from top left to bottom left.

4. Cut out the cover and fold along the dotted lines.

5. Slide the first and last pages into the cover pockets.

6. Cut out the matchbox cover, then write the title and decorate it. Finally, glue it onto a matchbox.

4. Pull out the inside corners of the front panel, as shown, to make a boat shape. Do the same to the other side.

5. Fold the left and right edges of the front flap forwards into the centre. Repeat to the back flap.

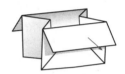

6. Fold the top flap forwards and the back flap backwards.

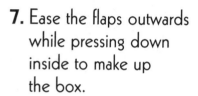

7. Ease the flaps outwards while pressing down inside to make up the box.

✏️ USE IT!

- Ask the class to choose an inanimate object, like a pencil or a shoe, that goes on holiday. Use the left-side pages for sentences and the right ones for matching illustrations.

- On each spread, children write and illustrate a different home improvement task done by the Three Little Pigs in their brick house, e.g., "We paint the walls green."

✏️ USE IT!

- Get the class to make an "I love" book. They can write "I love to run along the beach" or "I love to play in snow."

Choose any suitable book form using letter size paper. Place all the finished books inside the book box.

Whole-class book box

1. Fold the right and left long edges of a sheet of large size paper into the centre. Fold the paper widthways in half keeping the folds on the outside.

2. Fold the corners on the folded edge into the centre. Crease backwards. Unfold.

3. Fold the front and back bottom edges up to the top.

"Sarah's Birthday" by Sarah (aged 7). This miniature book was written and illustrated in the folded down form. To make further copies, the book is removed from its cover, opened flat and the cut sections are taped on the reverse to hold the sheet firmly together. As many photocopies as required can be made, and the copies are then folded, cut and refolded in the same manner as the original book.

24 – Lotus books

This origami base has a wide range of display possibilities, from a hanging book to a three-dimensional star. Use it for a class project and allocate one diamond-shaped panel per student.

Make the basic lotus book

1. Make a large square from a ledger size sheet of paper by folding the largest diagonal possible from it. Remove the rectangular strip.

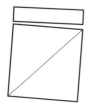

2. Turn the paper over. Fold the left edge forward to the right edge. Unfold. Fold the top edge forward to the bottom edge. Unfold.

3. Bring the top right and bottom left corners together. Doing this will make the shape start to close.

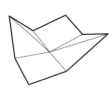

4. Bring the other two corners up to meet them. You will now have a small square.

5. Repeat steps 1 to 4 to create as many sections as you need for your project. Join the sections together. Glue each lotus base in the opposite direction to the one it is being attached to.

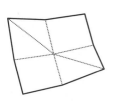

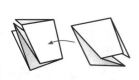

6. Two bases should look like this (see right) when glued together. You lose one diamond panel on each lotus by having the next base glued to it.

56

Decorative lotus book

1. Open the basic lotus form and fold it in half vertically. Fold the bottom corner diagonally forward. Fold it backward and unfold.

2. Turn it over and fold the top corner diagonally, as above. Repeat steps 1 and 2 on the horizontal crease.

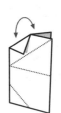

3. Fold the lotus up as before and then fold the triangular corners inward to complete the design.

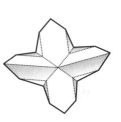

4. Join the sections together as described above.

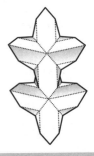

★ Helpful hint: Use strong paper for these hanging books.

Lotus star

1. Make four basic lotus books from ledger size paper as a base.

2. Join each lotus to the next one, pointing in the same direction.

3. Join the first and last panels together to make a star. Hold the edges together with a paper clip.

4. Make a hole near the top corner of the first and last panels and hang the star with string or strong cotton.

★ Helpful hint: To strengthen the star, glue cardboard covers to the first and last panels.

✏️ USE IT!

- Draw a large six-pointed star with a five-pointed star inside that and finally a four-pointed star inside that. Label each star.

- "This is my star." Each child decorates and captions a square panel before gluing it onto the lotus base.

Chinese magic envelope

1. Make the largest square possible from letter size paper. Fold it diagonally into a triangle. Fold in the left corner. Then, fold the right corner in an equal distance.

2. Fold back the end of the right flap.

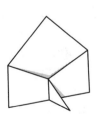

3. Open it up and press it flat to make a diamond shape.

4. Fold down the top corner and tuck it inside the diamond.

✏️ USE IT!

- Make this project to celebrate Chinese New Year. To the Chinese, red is good luck so use red paper. Children can decorate a panel with paint, pen work, collage and glitter before gluing it to the base.

- Make the basic lotus book, but add a dragon's head to it. Display as a meandering design, stapled to a large wall space or even hanging from the ceiling. Around this centrepiece, arrange Chinese "magic" envelopes, in which students have written wishes like "May you enjoy good health."

★ Helpful hint: If you have a central display area, attach work to the front and the back of a hanging lotus book.

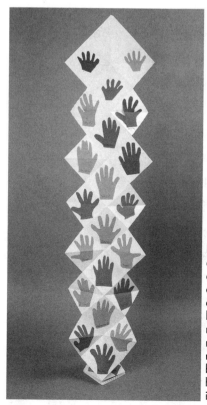

"Our Hands," a hanging lotus book. The teacher drew around one hand of each child in the class on colored paper. She then cut out and labelled each hand with the student's name. After assessing how many panels were required, the hanging book was made and the hands glued onto the individual sections.

25 – Firework books

These are called firework books because, as the book rises from its box, pop-ups open out like a pyrotechnic display and close again when folded down. The books fold down into small closed forms so they can be easily stored.

Make the basic firework book

1. Fold a margin on the bottom edge of portrait letter-size paper. Fold the top edge back down to meet the newly formed folded edge.

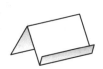

2. Fold the corners in diagonally to about a third of the way along the folded edge. Fold them backwards and forwards.

3. Unfold and crease the corners diagonally inwards.

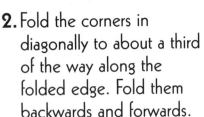

4. For the side pop-up flaps, make another page section as far as step 2 above. Remove the margin.

5. Fold the paper vertically at the first diagonal crease. Cut the paper as shown to make two panels.

6. Glue the panels each side of the base sheet.

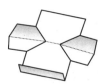

7. Join several sections together using the margins, which should always be at the bottom.

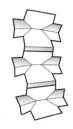

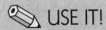
★ Helpful hint: Mounted work always looks more attractive than unmounted work.

Hanging project book

1. For the pop-ups: Make the basic firework book. Then make a duplicate base, remove the margin and cut out the pop-up flaps as shown.

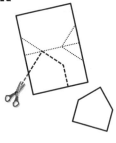

2. Glue the flaps to the bottom half of the side triangles. Then join several identical sections together, as before.

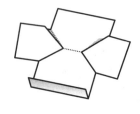

The tooth fairy

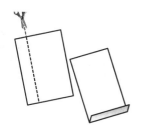

1. Remove a 6 cm (2 ¼ in.) strip from the long, left edge of a sheet of letter size paper. Fold a margin along the bottom edge.

2. Fold the top edge back down to meet the newly formed bottom edge.

3. Fold the corners on the top folded edge diagonally to the centre. Fold them backwards and unfold.

4. Fold the corners diagonally inwards.

5. For the wings, make a duplicate base and remove the margin. Cut the paper as shown.

6. Glue the wings to the top half of the side triangles on the base. Finally, join several sections together and fold them up as you did before.

Chinese fan book

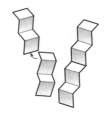

1. Cut a sheet of ledger size paper in half lengthways. Zigzag both pieces and join them together with tape at the back to make a long strip. Use one sheet of the paper for each child.

2. To make the fans, cut colored letter size paper widthways into four strips. Take one strip, fold it in half and unfold.

3. Fold the left and right edges of the strip into the centre and then into the centre again.

4. Open the strip and crease it into a zigzag.

5. Apply glue to the back of the first and last panels and glue it into place on a strip.

★ Helpful hint: Try hanging the books in different ways, e.g., making curves and s shapes.

Eight-page zigzag book template

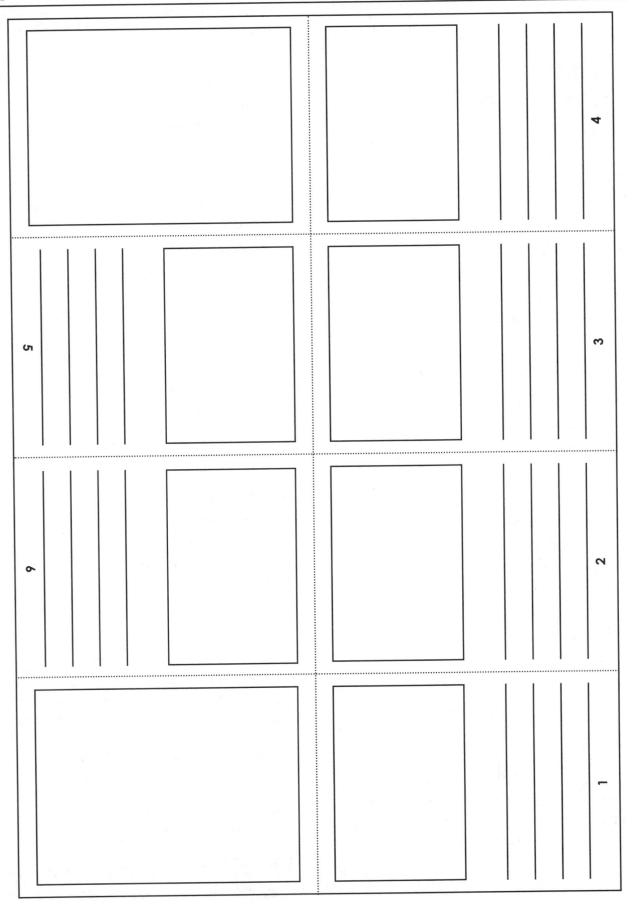

Origami book template

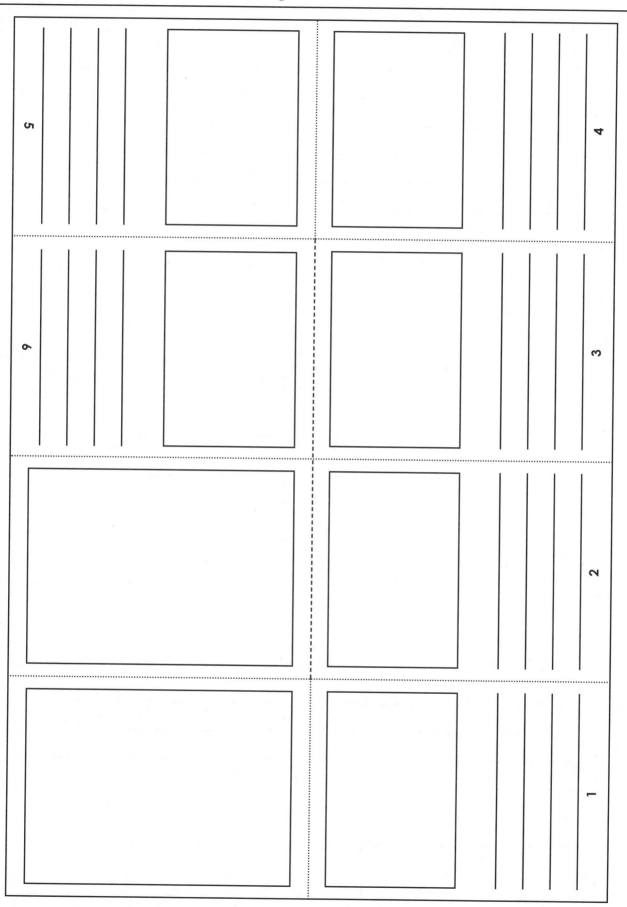

Four-page book template

1

2

16-page matchbox book template

Pages

Book cover

Matchbox cover